THE new

rules

of the

SISTERHOOD

Redefining and Restoring
the Power of Friendship

JANET BERNSTEIN

Published by The Every Heart Project, LLC of Carrollton, Texas

Copyediting by Ariana Scott

Proofreading by Catherine Paour and Heather Harbaugh

Cover design by Savvy Girl Media

Author photo by Vanessa Corral Photography

Special discounts for bulk sales (25 or more copies) are available.

Please contact info@everyheartproject.com.

IBSN: 9781091164895

PRAISE FOR JANET BERNSTEIN AND THE NEW RULES OF THE SISTERHOOD

"In this world of 'anything goes' that we live in what if a rule maker is born and heralded as a star? Well let us all join together and celebrate the shining star - Janet Bernstein. Bernstein has created a playbook for women to really help women....no secrets, no snarky, no snide, no sales - The New Rules of the Sisterhood. Since the beginning of time women have been wired to connect with one another. In this day and time it seems the playing field has gotten very complicated on how to do that in a serving, sharing, celebrating, caring, showing up, no conflict way. The New Rules of the Sisterhood will help women young or old create heart centered tribes no matter where they are in the world. Women once and for all will have a place where they genuinely feel like they belong from the moment they walk in the room....and in that room they will be able to stand tall and stand always in who they authentically are."

Debbie Mrazek

President, The Sales Company
www.The-Sales-Company.com

"Every woman needs to read this book! In Rules of the Sisterhood, Janet Bernstein uses wit, candor and personal anecdotes to examine the importance and challenges of female friendships. Her desire to help women form a 'sisterhood' and 'live by the code' is refreshing and admirable, reminding us that everyone wins by supporting and uplifting each other."

Janet George Flaig

Owner, Your Best Asset Bookkeeping, LLC
www.bookkeepersite.com

"After being a stay-at-home mom and homeschooler for 20+ years who recently started her own business, I didn't believe I belonged at a brunch for business women. Then Janet Bernstein stood up and started the meeting, telling everyone to 'leave your ego at the door' and encouraged us to share a challenge with the group. I did, and the rest is history. I found my tribe of loving, supportive women who have embraced and come along side me these last three years of my journey. I highly recommend The New Rules of the Sisterhood to anyone who is ready to learn what Janet has done to create such an amazing space for women to

gather, be encouraged, and grow by loving, supporting, and cheering on one another in today's business world."

Heather Harbaugh

Certified Aroma Freedom Technique Practitioner

www.Untethered.life

"The mission of The Every Heart Project speaks to my heart in so many ways. I was one of the women whom Janet Bernstein speaks about in the introduction of this book...the woman who lived in another state and saw a post on Facebook from a friend and wanted to catch the wave of what this amazing project is. It certainly wasn't hard to do. The rules of the Sisterhood embraced my interest from a distance, and I eventually found myself flying off to Dallas to attend the Third Annual Retreat. It was an amazing experience, and I felt closer to those sisters than the women in my own local networks here in California. Janet quickly became someone I really admire. I consider her not only one of my mentors, but a great coach, speaker, communicator, publisher, writer and even a dear friend. She has all the skills, strengths, service, smarts and savvy (and even an awesome singer) to lead this beautiful group of Sisters. Her mission to help women develop strong relationships and to

embrace their unique gifts was something I had been longing for. While I'm not able to be active in the local chapter, I walk alongside The New Rules of the Sisterhood, preparing myself to be part of her global

Mission. And, after reading this book, I am going to embrace the fact that I really do need to upgrade my bra! And I know whenever I travel to Dallas, there's always a seat at the table for me."

Catherine Paour, *The California Heart Sister*

My Hole Heart

"Janet Bernstein has a unique ability to lead women in achieving their highest potential while connecting with other women and forming true relationships. This book describes the steps necessary to do it all, and restore and rebuild the friendships in your life. I highly recommend every woman have this book in her library, and encourage each of us to eagerly gift a copy to another sister."

Josie Armijo Gamez

CEO, Lawncare by Josie
www.lawncarebyjosie.com

"Janet's book spoke to me on so many levels. I was excited to read about her taking on this difficult topic and bringing it to light with humor and sincerity. This is a must read for all women who are striving to be more and hear the message that we are a village of strong women who benefit from lifting each other up instead of tearing each other down."

Gina Doerr

Human Resources Manager

The book is dedicated to my Every Heart Sisters.

Thank you for saying YES to this journey, even though it isn't always the easiest road to travel. We are all better together and I'm thankful for each and every one of you.

ACKNOWLEDGEMENTS

Thank you to my editors and proofreaders:

Ariana Scott, my eldest daughter and soon-to-be college graduate. Your dedication to editing my creations warms my soul. When I said yes to becoming a young, single mom at the tender age of eighteen, I only dreamed I'd have a daughter like you as my friend one day. Dreams really do come true.

Catherine Paour, your relentless support for me from California was reason enough for me to keep going, even on the tough days. Thank you for reading, and re-reading, and re-reading (again) to make sure this book captured my intent and mission, and missed any of those annoying typos we both cringe at when we spot them in books.

Heather Harbaugh, you are a doll, especially for tolerating my obsessive comma usage. I guess I really like those little things. Thank you for the encouragement and support that always seem to arrive at the perfect time. I treasure our friendship and your gentle wisdom.

For my daughters: Ariana, Mya, Livia and **Sofia**... you are all authentic and amazing in your own way. My hope for each of you is to find your own unique path - the one that speaks only to the song in your heart and lights your soul on fire. Chase that always, and know that I am your biggest fan, obnoxiously cheering you on from the stands.

For my son, Joshua! Your tenacity is so admirable, and I cannot wait to see your future unfold. The Sisterhood in our household couldn't thrive without the best little brother supporting us all. Thank you for making sure our eye makeup is forever smeared from the tears of contagious laughter that fills our home.

Thank you to my amazing husband, Harold Bernstein, for encouraging me daily that this mission matters. Your commitment to me and our family is the reason I am able to write, create and dream as big as I could possibly want to, without fear you will ever discourage me. Thank you for reminding me of my inner *"Esther"* and *"Wonder Woman,"* especially on the days when the haters showed up.

Heart Sister Manifesto

Every Heart matters.

THIS IS OUR SISTERHOOD, COMPRISED OF BEAUTIFUL HEARTS FROM EVERY WALK OF LIFE.

We empower, elevate and equip each other for success.

WE SHOW UP.

We embrace the GIFTS OF OUR FELLOW SISTERS as well as our own.

We express our voices in harmony to promote inclusion, encouragement, hope and love.

We engage with ourselves, our sisterhood and our community.

We make room at the table for every woman.

We check our egos at the door, and arrive willing to serve.

EACH HEART IS WELCOME, UNAPOLOGETICALLY AND AUTHENTICALLY, QUIRKS AND ALL.

WE SEEK FIRST TO EXHIBIT EMPATHY OVER JUDGMENT.

We stand up for our sisters, and encourage others to do the same.

We believe the power of being surrounded by a tribe can transform the women in our world.

Every Heart has a story, a GIFT, a voice and a purpose.

Every Heart matters.

FOREWORD

How many times do you find yourself in situations that you don't understand and don't know how to change it?

We are all involved in groups and memberships and businesses where rules are made and so many are broken and no one tells you how to fix it... and the cycle continues. Where is the manual you need to create an environment where women want to be together, enjoy each other's company...or else move along?

When I started reading "The New Rules of the Sisterhood: Redefining and Restoring the Power of Friendship" I was wondering how there could be rules created for women that encourage being part of a sisterhood especially since I had just been unfriended, blocked and dismissed by someone I thought was a friend?

Well...Janet Bernstein did it and with grace, professionalism and some attitude. I giggled in parts and laughed out loud where I saw myself in some of her scenarios. We always remind ourselves that there isn't a manual for being a parent and wonder why no one has written one. Now you don't have to wonder where the how-to book is for redefining and restoring the power of friendship is...hopefully it's open on your desk so you can read it over and over again.

Thank you for letting us peek inside the curtain.

~ Judy Hoberman

President Selling In A Skirt & Walking on the Glass Floor
www.sellinginaskirt.com
www.walkingontheglassfloor.com

TABLE OF CONTENTS

**Praise For Janet Bernstein And
The New Rules Of The Sisterhood**..................iii

Acknowledgements........................ xi

Foreword xv

Introduction........................... xxi

RULE ONE: *Just Add a Leaf to the Table* 1

The Two Types of Women..................10

RULE TWO: *Be Unapologetically and Authentically You* 15

Drop the Mask 18

Tell the Truth, Always...................19

Be the Same Person Publicly and Privately 21

Don't Change for Anyone (or Anything) 23

Not Everyone You Lose is a Loss 24

The Good, The Bad and The Ugly 25

It's Contagious! 28

RULE THREE: *Be Inclusive*.................. 31

Keep Inviting.........................33

Don't Be Stingy 35

Diversity is Necessary...................37

Segregation Leads to Stereotypical Beliefs 38

Come As You Are......................39

Avoid the Bermuda Triangle 42

Bermuda Triangle Topic 1: Religion 43

Bermuda Triangle Topic 2: Politics 45

RULE FOUR: *Create Real Connections* 49

Far Outer Layer: Acquaintances 50

Outer Layer: Frenemies 51

Inner Layer One: Fun Friends 52

Inner Layer Two: Professional Friends 53

Innermost Layer: Good Friends 53

The Bullseye: Best Friends 54

Don't Give Up 58

Be a Secret-Keeper 59

RULE FIVE: *Check Your Ego At the Door* 61

How Can You Serve Your Sister? 63

Communication Care 65

Sisters Protect Their Sisters 66

Criticism is Deadly 67

Don't be a KIA 69

The Platinum Rule 70

Ego Vs. Heart 71

RULE SIX: *Show Up* 73

Integrity Matters 77

Choose Wisely 78

Missed Connections 79

Show Up for Each Other 81

Self-Care vs. Selfishness 82

The Guys Don't Struggle With This 83

RULE SEVEN: *Upgrade Your Bra* 85

    Marriage 88

    Career 89

    Friendships 90

RULE EIGHT: *Put Your Business Second (or Third)* 93

    It's Not All About You 94

    Be a Resource 95

    The First Meeting 96

    The Golf Course 98

    Don't Take Everything Personally 99

    Effing MLMs 100

RULE NINE: *Learn to Navigate Conflict* 105

    Straight to the Source 106

    Gossip Kills 108

    Your Reputation Depends Upon This 109

    Stay Out of the Middle 110

    When To Involve a Leader 112

    Be Brave Enough to Apologize First 115

RULE TEN: *Be a Giver, Not a Taker* 119

    Givers 120

    Takers 120

RULE ELEVEN: *Put the Damn Phone Down* 123

    Small Talk is Gone 125

    Important Conversations in Text 126

    Social Media 101 127

    Female Issues 127

    Marriage Issues 128

Vague-Booking...129

Politics or Religion...130

Food Pictures...131

RULE TWELVE: *More Empathy, Less Judgment*..............**133**

We have no right to judge anyone. 133

In the Name of Religion 134

Stop Perpetuating the Mental Health Stigma 136

Conclusion..**141**

Your Turn **143**

In Loving Memory of:..**145**

About the Author **147**

INTRODUCTION

This really shouldn't come as a surprise, but we need our female friendships. Studies have shown over and over again how much, as women, we need a tribe we can lean on, depend upon and truly grow with throughout life. That's why I created *The Every Heart Project*, a women's group with a mission to empower, elevate and equip women. If I'm being totally transparent, the group wasn't always called that. I didn't know how much the *"heart"* needed to be in this women's group at first. When I initially started the group in 2014, it was part of a national women's organization. I was a local chapter president, and began to host events to simply get women together on a regular basis. It started rather small; my first event only drew six women, and we met in a small, dark room in a family-owned bar-b-que restaurant in Carrollton, Texas. We met each month on the fourth Thursday. Eventually it grew to 20-30 women consistently, and I even added a brunch event each month during the week.

In 2016, I hosted a women's retreat, co-organized with one of my chapter members. We called the retreat *Every Heart Has a Story*, and it was focused on helping women find their story, own it, and tell it. Somehow we organized this powerful weekend and attracted 29 women to a local hotel in December, which is supposed to be the toughest month to gather women for a weekend event. Upon leaving the retreat, we were asked by all of the attendees to create more of those retreats, more opportunities to connect, and more heart. Thus, *The Every Heart Project* became the name of the group, and I officially resigned from the national women's organization and never looked back.

As I begin this book, I am currently preparing for our third annual retreat, Every Heart Has a Voice, happening in October 2018. By the time this book is published, dates will be revealed for our fourth retreat in 2019. The project has grown significantly, with an official membership program that was implemented this past year. My co-organizer from the first two retreats has officially stepped away from the project to pursue other endeavors, and the sky's the limit for these incredible Heart Sisters, as we appropriately call each other. I love the tribe we've formed, and getting to see the success and growth of so many heart-centered women is humbling, overwhelming and heartwarming. Some days I pinch myself, because this is truly my dream job, and I get excited before each and every event, workshop, happy hour or one-on-one meeting with a fellow sister. When we talk about living in our "zone of genius," it's clear I've definitely found mine.

But there's a piece of my heart that knows I can't simply focus on this local group and its inevitable growth. Creating unique and empowering events is certainly the goal for the project locally, but the ultimate mission is even greater than that. There are women all over my social media feeds who see and 'like' the posts about the project but never step foot at an event. There are women in other states (and countries) who have asked if there's an Every Heart Sister group in their area. The local group is only a small part of the mission. We have to view this project as an outreach, a lifeline for women everywhere who are searching for more from their female friendships. The women who attend each and every month are receiving heart-led leadership and forming life-long friendships, but there are women all over the world yearning for the same. How can we reach across borders and connect deeper and create an even larger sister Circle?

Well, that's where I come in.

I'm not saying the mission is mine and mine alone; I know in my heart this is a mission we all share as sisters. I hope you'll join me in this endeavor, and help me achieve it.

So how do we spread our message and foster a global movement of sisterhood? Well, we start with ourselves. It may seem anti-climatic, but stay with me. The problem isn't how many sisters we have or where they might be located. The problems arise when there's conflict or ignorance. We certainly can't create a global sisterhood if we are bickering with our own circle of sisters. But what if there was a code, like those powerful military codes we see on television, where they all *"live and die by the code!"* Yeah, like that, but we don't have to wear uniforms or do a fancy salute to each other. What if we had a set of rules that gave us our mission and guidelines and told us how to be better sisters? If we all followed the same set of rules, imagine how far our reach might extend. I picture a woman in another country who comes to our retreat and feels immediately at home when she walks in the door. The sisters who greet her embody the mission of the project, and they understand the rules. Instead of the immediate walls of protection that often get constructed before women form real connections with each other, these women can skip the formalities and cultivate relationships with new sisters. Call me crazy, but that's my mission.

Are you still in?

If you've gotten this far, you are probably wholeheartedly cheering for the mission and want to be part of a global Sisterhood! Or perhaps you think I've completely lost my mind and you want to simply keep reading out of curiosity. Either way, welcome aboard!

In this book, I promise to deliver my 'rules' to you in a fun, non-threatening manner, in hopes of creating a movement of women who are ready for deeper friendships and a life of purpose. You will probably laugh a lot, and I picture several of you adding in some *"amen, Sister"* responses, nodding along with me as you dive into my no-nonsense style of delivering these new rules. In all truth, there will likely be a few times your eyebrows raise and you cringe a little because there are some tough topics that need to be addressed as well. I know that going in, girlfriend, so take heart that we will get through it together. Part of my personal manifesto (yes, I actually have one of those) is *"I am comfortable getting uncomfortable."* We can't cover the fun and easy topics and skip the hard stuff, or things will never change. It's all part of the process. If you hit a part of the book that makes you want to throw it across the room, I encourage you to lean into that feeling (but don't throw the book) and dig further into yourself to figure out exactly what is triggering you to feel that way. Even better, grab your own circle of sisters and open it up for discussion. I guarantee you it will be enlightening, and it just may help you overcome those knee-jerk reactions or emotional impulses that sometimes get us into trouble anyway. Most of what I share comes from my own experiences or those from my local tribe. For privacy reasons, I refrain from giving exact names or too much information to identify a fellow sister. Those closest to me will probably recognize some of the stories, but they are meant to be shared in the spirit of learning, growing and understanding each other further. My intent is never to attack another sister, but rather to use these teachable moments to challenge us to be better and do better. If we want to start a movement of change, we have to admit our behaviors need to be changed. Before making a snap judgment when reading this book, really ask yourself how you can positively contribute to the conversation. It's easy to tear down people who think differently from us, but true strength comes from welcoming opposing ideas and being open to a new way of doing things. That's what this book is intended for, and I encourage you to come along for the journey.

Okay, so are you in?

Let's do this, Sister.

RULE ONE
JUST ADD A LEAF TO THE TABLE

"The problem isn't with the number of seats available at the table; the problem is we do not want to make room for anyone else to join us."

~Janet Bernstein

Let's be real, shall we? For years we have been told that there aren't enough seats at the proverbial table. Somehow there are plenty of seats for our male counterparts, but for whatever reason, seating is limited for women. Now don't get me wrong; I certainly recognize there's a glass ceiling and incredibly real challenges for women in the workplace. After spending 17 years in the corporate world, I found out the hard way that my two senior (male) partners could simply terminate my partnership agreement through a loophole in my contract.

And of course they created said contract. That experience taught me quite a bit about the uphill battle we often face as women trying to climb the ladder of success. But what if we've been fed a bunch of crap about there being limited seats or that women can't be friends and work together? What if all of the assumptions about women being catty or having issues with other women are just fabrications created to keep us from forming real relationships with each other?

Let that sink in a minute.

What if it's all a bunch of lies that we've been told to simply accept, and it doesn't have to be the truth? It's keeping us at arm's length from other women, or preventing those heart connections completely, stemming from a sense of competition and jealousy that we could easily change.

Let's face it; we know we need our girlfriends. We get together on a Thursday night, after finally booking a sitter, and spending an hour straightening our curly hair and wearing that new plum lipstick we purchased ages ago and lost in a sea of receipts and hair-ties in our bottomless purses. We actually put on real clothes, after having a brief internal debate about whether or not we can just wear our nice yoga pants and still leave the house. We end up in skinny jeans and one of those fun, open-shoulder tops and show up ready to enjoy the night. We have an amazing time filled with laughter, hugs and sometimes tears. But we are always holding back a little when it comes to forming those tight relationships, a part of us not trusting the motives of other women. We've all been burned before. Subconsciously, we've built walls around our hearts to protect us from the mean girls. We hide behind past hurts and broken promises, always ready to spew the heartbreaking stories when someone asks us why we won't join a certain group or tag along to a movie with a small group of women. We proudly wear our pain like hard-earned Girl Scout badges, citing it as the reason we are the way we are, and the idea of changing that behavior scares most of us to death. So we perpetuate the cycle. Our past hurts prevent us from forming those heart connections in the future, or at least forming them easily.

I used to be this way, too. I'm not gonna lie. I used to say those same things, like *"Women are catty"* or *"I don't trust many women."* I only had a few close friends, and then one day I woke up around the age of thirty and realized I had one good friend, and a handful of prospects on a "maybe list." If I had a rough day, I didn't have someone who would drop everything and bring me my favorite chocolate peanut butter ice cream with caramel syrup and help me eat it while I cried the ugly cry and watched Pretty Woman for the 500th time. If I wanted to host a dinner party, I drew a complete blank when I thought about who would actually fill those seats. I certainly knew other women and had worked with them or gone to church with them. But I didn't truly know them. I didn't know what made them scared or made them sad. I didn't have any idea how hard their childhoods were, or if they had suffered being raised by a mother with a mental illness, like I had. I often wondered if any of them questioned their decisions to work in a particular industry, or if they constantly daydreamed about starting their own businesses. When I realized I missed out on forming these true friendships, I discovered I had spent the last several years pouring all of my love and time into my family. Don't get me wrong; I love my family. I have three kids, and I don't regret spending a lot of time with them when they were little. But as they started to get older, I'd be left sitting at the computer at night, writing or aimlessly scrolling through social media, only to realize I missed human interaction. But not just *human* interaction. Truthfully, I missed interaction with women. I would see pictures on my news feeds of acquaintances meeting for wine and cheese tastings or girls' nights, and my heart ached to have that for myself, as well as for other moms just like me. I wanted to have a group of women who could drop everything once a year and go to Mexico on a girls' trip. I wanted a tribe that I could invite over following a crappy week and say *"chick flick at my house!"* I craved it, which told me there were other women craving the same thing.

Then in 2011, I found myself in the midst of a divorce. Everything I had spent years building came crashing down upon me, and my first marriage dissolved before my very eyes. That's when I realized just how much I needed those female friends. I began to reach out to a few women I knew and make time for coffee or lunch. I loved it. I had missed it, and I wanted more of it. Not too long after, I was selected to lead a local chapter for a national women's organization. I just knew this was my chance to create a women's group where members felt uplifted, supported and inspired. My Power Brunch became known as one of the most powerful women's events in Dallas, as well as a safe place for a woman to share challenges or needs she may have in her business and the rest of the room would act as an unofficial board of advisors, offering advice, solutions or ideas. My personality type seemed to be absolutely perfect for this format because I could moderate the comments and keep things moving at a nice pace. Sometimes I had to cut women off, especially if they became really long-winded or got off topic. In the beginning, I would apologize for interrupting them, but over time I grew more confident and just kept it moving. To this day, many of our first time guests often compliment me on the format and pace of the brunch, and thank me for keeping things moving quickly and efficiently. It was during this time that I met my second husband, Harold, and his support for my women's group was invaluable. He totally understood why it was necessary and encouraged me even on the dark days. He would listen to me ramble on and on about how amazing that day's brunch was or the magic that happened in that room. He never grew tired of watching me light up when talking about the work I was doing.

My focus for the brunch is to create a supportive space for women to let their guard down and allow other women to pour into them. For many, this is the first time they've ever participated in anything like this, and so often they are leary of the event, or even of me. Once they attend a few times, they may say things like, "Wow, you really do care about us, don't you?" And yes, I do care. I care deeply about the lives and hearts of women. Many evenings I come home from events and feel heartbroken over something happening to a fellow sister. I may pray over them or send them supportive texts during tough times. We need to feel celebrated and welcomed. We need to know that we matter. Having another woman tell us we look beautiful, after spending the day feeling like we aren't enough, can change the course of a life. Even if our parents loved us, and even if our husbands love us, we need our sisters. Women building up other women boosts confidence, not just in each other, but in the sisterhood in general.

Think about when you were in high school standing next to your best friend by your lockers in the school hallway. I was a nineties' kid, so I was likely sporting JNCO, wide-legged jeans and black, Doc Martens boots, a choker, and an uncomfortable black bodysuit that snapped at the crotch (who thought this was a good idea?) and a men's flannel shirt. Can you picture this now? Now imagine the prettiest and most popular girl in school walks by. Once she passes you both, what's the dialogue between you and your best friend? Do you both smile and talk about how gorgeous she is and how you saw her rescue a baby squirrel from a burning tree on the way home yesterday? Probably not. The immediate response, though unfortunate, was probably not a nice one. We have been conditioned to criticize other women, especially if they have something we want or exhibit integrity or good deeds.

This may start in middle school, but the same behavior continues to happen when we become adults. If no one ever smacks us in the head and says, *"Ladies, cheer for her and we all win!"* then we just keep repeating this dangerous cycle. And we all lose. The new rule for sisterhood is to cheer for each other, and cheer loudly. If we see a fellow sister achieve something, we should be the first to congratulate her. Comment on her posts, share them, attend their events, and only speak positive and empowering words! Seriously, we have nothing to lose.

I feel as though I need to repeat that last part for those in the back of the room...

When we cheer each other on, we have NOTHING to lose.

Last year I was invited to an awards ceremony, recognizing several women entrepreneurs in the Dallas area for their achievements and reach. I found out a couple of my friends were nominated and I wanted to attend to support them as they were recognized. I mentioned this to a friend when she asked what I was doing that evening. When I told her about the awards, she said to me, *"Aren't you upset you weren't nominated with all that you've done to bring women together?"* I smiled and said, *"No, I'm not upset at all. I don't do what I do for awards, and I certainly recognize there are other women in this space doing amazing things. I can't wait to celebrate the women I know who were recognized!"* She seemed shocked and then mentioned how she would not be attending because she wasn't even considered for the awards. I found our whole exchange a bit sad and realized she clearly doesn't understand the rules of sisterhood. Cheering for another woman's success never hurts your own chances of success. In fact, if you believe all of that law of attraction stuff, gratitude and positivity only help you receive more. This woman refusing to celebrate other women actually could prevent her from experiencing her own success. Let's take it a step further... what if when she is selected for some sort of award, there's no one there cheering her on either? This is a perpetual cycle that must be broken. Stop listening to the haters and the Negative Nancys who are telling you that you have to hate the pretty ones or the smart ones, or the leaders. Just stop. Get your envy or jealousy in check, put your big girl panties on, and start cheering for each other.

9

The Two Types of Women

I know I'm going to catch some flack for this, and I really don't care, but I think there are two types of women. The first type are the champions of other women, and they are truly my favorite. They cheer for you when you succeed and show up to your awards ceremony with flowers or a card. In fact, they may be obnoxiously shouting your name as you take the stage, possibly even embarrassing you a bit as others are whispering, *"Wow, she's popular."* They comment on all of your posts, share them, and support you both to your face and to the faces of others. They say *"Great job, girlfriend!"* and actually mean it, and they defend you if someone talks badly about you. These women know that it's okay to celebrate the success of other women and that it will never dampen your own by doing it. They don't believe that everything is a competition, and they are probably a lot freakin' happier because of that. These women are the ones you want to go to brunch with because they won't think twice about telling you there's a piece of spinach stuck in your teeth. They don't hesitate to lean over and tuck in your t-shirt tag, or let you know that little '1X' clear size sticker is still stuck to the butt of your new favorite pair of leopard print leggings. These ladies will look after you like, well, sisters. And that's gold.

The other type of woman is the one who watches and smiles, but secretly bad-mouths you to others. She may comment on your posts with *"You go girl!"* but then tells everyone they know that you don't deserve the recognition, or that you're not who you say you are. These women are often acting out of jealousy or envy, but it may not appear as obvious to others. Often times these women appear to be kind-hearted and supportive and may even be known as a life coach or expert in their field. Those are the ones you have to watch out for because everyone else sees them as amazing, until they get burned. The challenge with this type of woman is that often you may not truly see the real side until something bad happens. In my case, I started working closely with a woman I thought was a really supportive person. I discounted my services, offered to help her build her new business, and ended up getting burned. I found out that the entire time she was spreading negativity and lies about me to mutual friends. It wasn't until someone told me what was happening and I confronted her that I started to see the truth. I was heartbroken, but then I started seeing her do it to other women in our circle. These types of women only care about their own success and achievements and see other women achieving as competition. It may not be obvious at first, if you are friends with this type of person, until you have a major achievement and they attempt to make you feel as though you shouldn't be proud of it. They will share little comments such as, *"Oh, you're releasing another book, even though your last one was just finished a few months ago? You know marketing a book is a lot of work, right?"* They may seem as though they are being helpful, but their motives aren't pure. *"Wow, you sure record a lot of Facebook videos, don't you? I guess you don't worry about being seen with messy hair or no makeup, huh?"* Not helpful. Not supportive. The motive is to sprinkle your head with doubts and make you question your purpose or actions. No bueno. A true friend, and a true champion of women, would encourage you and be proud of your accomplishments. Don't be fooled by the two-faced women in your circle, even if it seems like they know everyone or have clout. They might, but they will use it to hurt you, and you're probably better off without them in your life. Trust me, girl; it ain't worth it. I ended my friendship with that bad-mouthing friend I talked about earlier. It was difficult, and I even lost a few mutual friends because of it. I chose to keep my mouth shut when asked what happened because I didn't want to perpetuate that cycle of gossip or the notion that women are evil. Her behavior only supported that opinion, and I am rebuilding and restoring female friendships and relationships. In the end, I sacrificed my own chance to speak up and be heard so the mission could continue to be the center of attention. At the end of the day, my priority is the mission. I'm a big girl, and I can handle my own hurt feelings. And I did, silently, without involving others.

We truly are stronger together. If a group of women are at an event and another woman begins to talk negatively about someone else, there is power in numbers. A group can immediately shut down bad behaviors, which is why it's imperative that you surround yourself with the right people. Are you sitting at a table with women who uplift, inspire and empower you? Or are you sitting with a table with women who criticize and judge you and others? Choose wisely.

The problem isn't the number of seats at the table. We have the power to add a leaf to that table and bring in more chairs from the garage. There's always room for more.

RULE TWO
BE UNAPOLOGETICALLY AND
AUTHENTICALLY YOU

"Authenticity is the daily practice of letting go of who we think we are supposed to be and embracing who we are."

~Brene Brown

I firmly believe that many of the miscommunications and conflicts in the sisterhood happen simply because someone isn't being authentic. When we deny who we truly are, we make decisions that are based on false truths or lies. There is only one you. You are unique, and you have all sorts of fun quirks and traits that make up your personality. In my case, I tend to stick my tongue out when my husband looks longingly into my eyes and tells me how beautiful I am or how much he loves me. It's not that I *don't* want him to say those things. I just like to insert comical moments into intense circumstances. Yeah, some might say it's weird. I'm okay with that. I like to burst into song when someone says a sentence that resembles a famous musical or my favorite movie. I also mimic other accents, sometimes out of habit, and that's gotten me into trouble before. There's a beautiful sister in my tribe who is from New Zealand and has a gorgeous accent; I once imitated her at an event (though thankfully not on stage) and I think I may have offended her a bit. I apologized. I don't do it out of disrespect or making fun. I just love doing voices and playing roles. Perhaps it was my many years in musical theatre? Whatever the reason, it's part of who I am. The moment I start trying to suppress those personality traits and behaviors, resentment and discontent start to creep in. That inner voice starts to whisper things like, *"Don't show them who you truly are, or you might scare them!"*

In today's world, women are often caught in a tough place when it comes to authenticity. They want to show up and be real, but they are also trying to be politically correct, tolerant, open-minded, friendly, and everything else they are being told is necessary. And if they are trying to run a business that's fueled by social media, it's even more difficult. They may post something they feel is authentic and true, only to see zero engagement on their feed, only to result in questioning their decisions. The true problem, though, is that we are listening to others about how we *should* be instead of just showing up as who we are.

I remember a few years ago I found myself at a networking event and an 'expert' spoke about women and their presence, along with clothing choices. The speaker was a former beauty queen, with a size 2 figure and quite beautiful. As she spoke, however, I became somewhat annoyed with her, and not because she was gorgeous! I was annoyed because she was superficial. She spoke in a voice that was clearly not her normal voice, and every move she made on stage looked like a pose in a magazine, arching her back and flipping her hair around like a swimsuit model. Then she started giving advice to women about what to wear or not to wear to networking events. Black was bad. Red high-heeled shoes were good. A pop of color was necessary. But here's the thing I realized... her advice was for herself. It really didn't apply to the majority of the women in the room. I love black clothes, and I hate heels. And showing up to an event wearing something that truly wasn't 'me' wasn't going to help me with confidence or presence. I'm also considered to be a *'plus-size'* woman - many of her clothing recommendations just didn't seem applicable to women over a size 10 or 12, in my opinion. We are all made differently, and giving advice like that can be irresponsible. Her platform had potential, but her message wasn't authentic; it was not effective. Perhaps in a room of similar women, she might have struck a chord with many. In this room, not so much. It's hard to relate to someone who isn't being authentic.

Drop the Mask

When women first set foot at our Every Heart Project events, I usually notice there's a mask they are proudly sporting. Often times, it's just a protective layer they've decided to keep to prevent others from seeing too much too soon. I remember one sister who walked in one time and said, *"Hi, I'm just here to meet some new people, but I don't make friends easily, so I'm not expecting much."* Wow. I saw that as a challenge and made sure to introduce her to some of my amazing tribe. Two years later, she is now an active member of the group, and one I often see commenting on the other sisters' posts and cheering them on. I think we tend to put these masks on as a way of protecting ourselves from others, but if anything, they are preventing others from being blessed by who we truly are underneath. Drop the mask. Be proud of who you are and how far you've come to get here. Let others see you and love you. Truth be told, I think one of the reasons I have been successful in building this tribe is because I can see past those masks and help these women take them off. It's certainly not an easy task, but it's necessary. When new women come to our group, I immediately identify if they are introverts, scared of other women, intimidated, or just heartbroken. I try to figure out what they need most to heal and move forward in their lives. Sometimes it's connecting them with a fellow sister that I just know will be a heart connection. Sometimes it's buying their product or service to support them or simply introducing them to someone who may need their product or service.

Tell the Truth, Always

First of all, let's talk about little white lies. They are the lies that many say don't count. They are the little passes we give our husbands or spouses that allows them to say *"Of course not"* when we ask them if we look fat in that dress we haven't worn since our twenties. I would venture to say we do this with our girlfriends as well when they ask things like, *"Even though I haven't washed my hair in a week, it doesn't really look dirty, does it?"* Well, yes it does, Becky. But what good comes of that? So, yes, the little white lies are probably okay in many cases. But other lies matter. If your fellow sister asks you, *"When I said she looked stupid, was I wrong?"* That is precisely the time to start telling the truth. If your motive is to tear another person down, that's when you're doing wrong, and that's when we need to correct each other in a loving way. If a fellow sister calls you and asks you, *"Do you think I should start a blog about wanting to be a rapper?"* It's time to tell the truth. No, Susan, you probably won't be the next Nicki Minaj. Sorry, girlfriend. Don't let another sister go down some insane path without helping her out a bit. If she only hears *"Go for it, girlfriend!"* from every single friend, then later she's going to wonder why no one told her the truth. Yeah, I know that's a silly example. It's meant to be silly. When we are talking about telling the truth, it's just about being authentic and not lying to our sisters. Don't say, *"I can't go to your event on Friday because my mother-in-law is forcing me to go Tupperware shopping with her."* Just tell the truth. *"Girl, sorry but I will miss your event on Friday, but I wish you lots of success!"* Don't lie. You don't even have to give specific reasons why. Being authentic means you aren't afraid to just speak truth and be okay with the consequences. Maybe you do give specifics, but in a loving way. *"Sorry, Jill, but I don't like that weight-loss coffee you are selling now. But have a great time!"* I think it's time we start telling the truth. The lies are what get us into trouble.

Be the Same Person Publicly and Privately

This one is probably the foundation of a truly authentic life. When someone meets you for the first time, and then months later when they see you on television or hear you on the radio... are you the same person? This is a big deal to me because I'm often speaking on stage or recording lots of videos online. When I run into people in real life, I love hearing, *"Wow, you're exactly like you were in that video!"* or *"Your personality is so genuine!"* and even, *"I feel like I already know you so well!"* Those are compliments to me because it means I'm showing up authentically for my audience. Think about your favorite celebrity. Imagine running into them at the local movie theater, only to realize they're a total jerk. Perhaps they spill a drink on someone and cuss out another patron or laugh at a special needs boy in the theater. Suddenly, you're probably not as big of a fan. In fact, I would say you probably wish you could take back all of those hours you spent thinking they were so awesome. Just sayin'.

I know a lot of women are overly concerned with keeping their public life and private lives separate. I get that. But in today's world, you can attempt to separate those lives, but it is virtually impossible to be different in each life. If you're happy-go-lucky in public and negative and dark in private, that's probably going to bleed over into real life eventually. Just be you. Don't stress about what others want to see or who they want you to be. It's a lot easier if you just own it. If you're the class clown, own that. If you're the cheerleader who loves to encourage, show it. If you're philosophical and deep, go for it. Whatever you do, just be true to who you truly are, and life is a lot easier. Don't be afraid to lose friends. If they don't love you for who you are, then they don't love YOU.

I remember last year I went to see this documentary of a fellow trailblazing woman in the empowerment world who is changing the lives of women through books, videos, podcasts and more. She also hosts conferences with hundreds of women, and I was watching closely to glean any ideas or inspiration for our third annual retreat that was approaching. I noticed when she took the stage for the first time, she came out wearing jeans and tennis shoes. My mouth dropped and I had a huge realization. At the past two retreats, both of which I co-hosted with a fellow sister, I had felt pressure (from within) to dress a certain way. My co-facilitator was a size zero, had a fabulous wardrobe of business clothes, and a never-ending collection of gorgeous high heels and accessories. I tried to match, as best I could, wearing sweater dresses and heeled boots, and even tried the "business casual" attire I had stowed away in my closet from my corporate days. I don't think I ever truly felt like *me* on stage during those events. Don't misunderstand me; my fellow sister didn't force me to dress this way, but I chose to apply that pressure to myself. After watching that documentary, I immediately pulled out my journal and wrote, *"Dress like me for the retreat."* Sure enough, a few months later, I smiled as I took the stage in jeans and bright red Converse tennis shoes. I was on top of the world and felt as though I was being my most authentic self.

Don't Change for Anyone (or Anything)

When we talk about authenticity, especially in the sisterhood, it means just being you. Stop apologizing for being too loud, or too quiet, or too silly, or too friendly. If someone tells you that you are too much, it simply means you are too much for them. It has absolutely nothing to do with you. Let that crap go and keep on being you. We can probably all think of a few examples of when we dated someone as a teenager or back in our twenties when we tried to be something we weren't. We pretended to love football, even though we couldn't stand it. We agreed that pineapple had no place on pizza, though we secretly loved Hawaiian pizza. We attempted to conform to someone else's needs or desires, and it never worked, at least not long-term. When we disguise who we truly are for a relationship, we begin to resent the other person. The same holds true in the sisterhood. If someone says to you, *"You can come, Susie Q, but you can't make jokes,"* then that means they know who you truly are, and they want you to change. Just say no. And don't go! If they can't accept you for who you truly are, jokes and all, then they don't deserve you. One of our sisters in the tribe has this hilarious giggle, and it usually slips out at the most inappropriate times. It's truly part of what makes her unique and what makes her, well, her. Although at times it's awkward when that laugh makes its debut, we recognize that's part of that sister. And she is welcome at our events, always, without a disclaimer. Remember, if anyone tells you that you need to change, it probably has more to do with them than you. Just keeping being your quirky, fun self. Don't show up as less of you simply because they can't handle the real you.

Not Everyone You Lose is a Loss

So, this might be hard for some of you recovering people pleasers, but not everyone you lose is a loss. By being your most authentic self, it might be too much or not enough for someone. They may speak up and make comments like, *"You're so funny, but I wish you'd tone it down when we're with other friends."* Umm, no thank you. I'm not going to tame my personality for your comfort. Now, I would be happy to make some changes if I offend you in some way. But just because I'm blunt or loud or whatever adjective makes you uneasy, that's not a good enough reason for me to change. Sorry. If everyone loves you, I would challenge you to say you aren't being authentic. We aren't meant to click with everyone; it's just not realistic. If someone rubs you the wrong way, don't feel bad about it! Just limit your interaction with them and understand there's something off there. Over time, that may dissipate, but don't force it. If you "lose" a friend because you were simply being yourself, they were never really a friend in the first place.

The Good, The Bad and The Ugly

We aren't all perfect. In fact, none of us is perfect. We all have crappy days, and we all have days when the last thing we want to do is deal with others. Many of our sisters are introverts and may find more healing in being alone than gathering with us extroverted ones. That's okay. The mission of The Every Heart Project is truly to connect women's hearts. That means overlooking some of the not-so-wonderful attributes we may exhibit. We have sisters who habitually show up late to events. Though it's a personal pet peeve of mine, especially since I'm planning these events and feel as though someone who misses 30 minutes of it is truly missing out on something amazing, I have to overlook it. We have women who suffer from crippling anxiety and depression, which may result in them missing events altogether. It always makes me sad to see that last-minute text, saying, *"Sorry I just can't make it tonight."* Even though they probably needed the time with sisters more than anything in the world, there was nothing I could do to help them when they didn't show up. And I just have to support them and tell them they were missed. Authenticity isn't just for the women; it's for me as their leader as well. It doesn't mean that I don't express my disappointment when they don't show up or when they cause drama. It means I do it with love. I can call out specific behaviors without alienating the sister. I can continue to lead by example and hope others do the same. But encouraging authenticity is truly about telling these incredible sisters that they are still welcome in our tribe. Even if they screw up. Even if they missed two events, after saying they'd be there. Even if they had a horrible day and they know it's going to take at least an hour at the event to shake themselves out of it. It's okay. That's the power of authentic leadership. We all have bad days. Don't miss out on the blessings of the sisterhood just because you are beating yourself up. That's actually the most important time to plug back into the tribe. When you feel yourself drifting, extend your hand and ask for help. One thing I love most about our local tribe is the support when someone asks for help. When one sister's parents were in a horrific car accident, a dozen sisters took turns bringing dinners each night to her family. When the daughter of a sister had an unexpected financial crisis in another country, many pitched in a few dollars to help cover the immediate need and get the daughter home. One of our members owns a charity that helps cancer patients with financial support and resources. When there was a need for an upcoming event, more than 30 women got together and volunteered their time and brainstormed ideas for fundraising, event planning and more.

There's an incredible sister in my tribe who truly struggles with depression, and it manifests in her signing up for events and then never showing up. She always feels horrible about it after, but then does it again the following week. Recently, I challenged her to break the cycle. I encouraged her to keep her promises to herself and to celebrate even the little wins. We brainstormed on some ideas of how to stay on track, even during tough weeks, and how to find some accountability partners in the tribe to help. But none of this would be possible if she didn't just say, *"I'm struggling and I need help."* The moment she did that, she felt the tribe step in. That's the magic. And once again, it only happens when we take off those masks, let our guard down and be authentic and honest.

It's Contagious!

Authenticity is truly one of the most contagious things ever. It's like that end-of-the-world virus they love to feature in zombie films, where we are all infected no matter what. When you show up being unapologetically you, you allow others to do the same. Sisters who are trying to find their own voices may suddenly feel that little nudge to spread their wings, especially after seeing you do the same. Don't be afraid to show up. You never know who you are inspiring. I love the stories I hear of sisters who left a lunch or coffee date with a fellow sister, completely fired up and ready to rock. They will often use phrases like, *"She inspired me that starting over at any age is possible,"* or *"Hearing her story of overcoming truly made me realize I'm ready to do this!"* Imagine if we all got out of our own heads and just started being authentic and showing everyone our true selves? For some, it may sound kind of scary, but think of the incredible ripple effects! I often talk about how my kids are watching my every move. If I'm proud of who I am and proud of what makes me unique, they are going to follow in my footsteps. But if I criticize myself or hide my true personality, what does that teach them to do in return? All behavior can be contagious. It's your choice which behaviors you adopt. Choose wisely!

RULE THREE
BE INCLUSIVE

*"Diversity is being invited to the party;
inclusion is being asked to dance."*

~Verna Myers

Do you know that feeling that comes when you find a hole-in-the-wall restaurant and discover they make the best guacamole and homemade tortillas you've ever had? Plus, their prices are unbelievably low, and there was virtually no wait to be seated. As you contemplate posting a pic of your gorgeously gourmet dish, you suddenly fear that your little gem of a restaurant is going to become instantly famous from your Instagram posts and you'll never be able to get a table again. You picture showing up on a Saturday night, only to find an hour wait and the prices have increased. Your favorite server has changed his schedule to only work on Friday because now he makes so much in tips he can adopt five dogs and three orphans from Cambodia and spend his free time with them. So you keep it to yourself. You show up every two or three weeks for your favorite meal, never telling a soul about this incredible place. Imagine if everyone else who frequented the restaurant did the same. One day you pull up to the front, shocked at how there are no cars in the parking lot, only to see a 'closed' sign on the door. You find out they went out of business. But how could that happen? Their guacamole was incredible! And those tortillas! How could this happen? It's because no one shared the amazingness with others, so it never grew to all it could be. The same is true with a great sisterhood. If you never tell the women in your life who desperately need it, they will never know the blessings that await them.

I've shared the details of The Every Heart Project with just about every woman I've ever met. I tell everyone I meet about it, and I post about it almost daily on social media. I invite all the women in my newsfeed to my events, and I keep inviting them, even if they say they're busy or out of town, or whatever. Why do I do that?

Because they need this. I don't care if they are one of the "mean girls." They need this tribe. Besides, even the mean girls eventually change their ways, or they move on when they can't spread the hate they are used to spreading in their other groups. No, my tribe really isn't for everyone, but everyone is welcome. Often I will receive a message from a member, letting me know she was going to invite someone, but she seemed like she wasn't a good fit. While I understand the decision, I also encourage them not to make assumptions, unless they have really good reasons to believe this lady wouldn't find joy in our group. Sometimes, women come to our group and act like mean girls. They gossip and spread lies and immediately spam the other women with their latest business venture. But over time, many of these women evolve. They realize they weren't showing up authentically, and they remove the mask and become a true sister. That's what it's all about. So I encourage our members to just invite everyone. You never know who might be the next sister to bring your family a meal or pitch in to help someone you love.

Keep Inviting

I get all sorts of excuses when I invite women to our events and retreats. *"Oh, I travel a lot."* Awesome. How about traveling to my event? It's cheaper than airfare. *"I have small children.*" So you never go out of leave the house? That's cool. *"My children are in sports."* That's wonderful. So they play every single night of the week now? When my husband and I coached softball, that didn't seem to be possible. But here's the deal. These excuses may all be completely valid. They might be absolutely and positively true for you. But they also might be little self-imposed excuses preventing you from establishing one night per month that you dedicate to only you. That's the reason we host our Elevate event on the fourth Thursday of the month. It's so our women can slap that on their Google calendars and plan for it. Why is that so hard for us as women to do? Why are we totally okay with saying *"little Johnny has baseball every Saturday morning and Tuesday night,"* and *"precious Veronica has dance every Tuesday and Thursday."* But we don't dedicate any time to ourselves. Our husbands or boyfriends can say *"I'm playing golf on Saturday with the guys from the office,"* and they rarely cancel. They make it a priority and show up. I keep inviting women because one day they are going to realize they need this and they are going to say yes. Or, they're just going to get sick and tired of me asking, and they are going to finally say *"Okay, okay, Janet, I'll go to your women's thing!"* Then, they're hooked. (Picture me with a sneaky facial expression, rubbing my hands together with that Disney villain laugh.) They instantly feel the magnetic power of the sisterhood and the sense of belonging, and they begin to realize it's the missing piece of their puzzle. Or it's the first time since their divorce that they had a good laugh. Or their very best friend or sister passed away recently, and this is the first time they felt as though they could get close to another woman again. Or they lost their job last month and have been searching for their purpose, only to realize it after connecting with a fellow sister who went through the same thing. There's magic that happens at those meetings. And that's why I won't stop inviting them. This restaurant won't be closing if I have anything to do with it.

Don't Be Stingy

In 2016, when the group was technically still a part of the national women's organization, I decided to host a retreat, which I co-facilitated with another member. We had 29 women show up and spend the weekend with us in a local hotel, enjoying everything from s'mores on Friday night, to a pajama party on Saturday night. We also poured into them nuggets of wisdom and support related to owning and sharing their own powerful stories. I had just completed my first solo book at the time, *"Pizza On the Floor,"* my memoir of growing up with a mother with

Borderline Personality Disorder. The process of writing my book was so empowering and therapeutic, and I wanted to provide that wisdom to our tribe. The weekend was absolutely incredible, and we knew we'd have to do it again the following year. We gave the ladies a survey to share their feedback and wishes as we planned the next retreat. Some of the responses were, *"I'm concerned we will lose the intimacy if we grow into a bigger group"* or *"A larger group means less connecting."* Here's the problem. We are being stingy when we don't share something incredible with the world. When a church starts to grow and reach more people, they don't close the doors when it's full. They build a bigger church. It's not up to us how many hearts we reach. It's out of our control. If every single retreat comes and I only have 40 or 50 women, that's okay. But if 100 show up, that's telling me I am meant to help 100 women that weekend. In turn, those 100 women will touch hundreds more with the newly open hearts and gems they've gleaned from our retreats. Our responsibility is to share the amazing experiences with others so they can decide if they want to be a part of it or not. Remember, add a leaf to the table.

Diversity is Necessary

I'm a firm believer that you should be surrounding yourself with people who challenge you to be better and inspire you to achieve more. Often times, we forget that people with other life experiences are more likely to affect us in our journeys than those in the same circle. For example, if you have always wanted to become an international speaker, your immediate friends who have never left the state are not likely to be the ones to encourage you and challenge you in your purpose. There's a great quote I recently heard, but have no idea who first said it: *"We have to stop asking people for directions who have never gone where we want to go."* If they are scared to fly, they aren't going to be able to teach you how. If they have never taken a leap of faith, you certainly can't hold their hand as you jump. Accept that and be open to expanding your circle. Those who have walked different paths can often open our eyes to new perspectives and ideas. The same is true in our sisterhood. If you look around your table at lunch and notice everyone looks just like you, it's likely you are not being challenged to be better or grow. We need to start opening our hearts and doors to those of different faiths, different nationalities and beliefs.

Segregation Leads to Stereotypical Beliefs

I remember being in high school, finding myself at another new school after moving yet again. My first day at the new school, I felt very much an outsider. I didn't know anyone, and all of these kids had grown up together, attending all of the same schools since kindergarten. I wandered into the lunch room and found an empty table to start eating lunch. Within minutes, I was joined by several girls who let me know this was "their table." I apologized and started to stand up, but was immediately told, *"Oh, you can stay. You look nice. Wait, what are you?"* I wasn't exactly sure of the question. What was I? She got annoyed with my lack of response. *"Are you Hispanic or White?"* Oh, race. Okay, that was interesting. *"I guess I'm White."* She looked even more annoyed with my response. *"Either you're White or not. There's no guessing, unless you're adopted."* I didn't care for this conversation. My last school was incredibly mixed and tolerant, and I felt sad now as I found myself at this table of girls. I didn't respond again, and she continued, *"Over there are the Mexican kids, and they are all dangerous and rude. That table over there are the Black kids, and they skip school a lot and do drugs. And that table is the football team, and they are kind of dumb, but they have the best parties. And this is the*

White side of the cafeteria. So if you cross that line, you will not be a part of our group."

This whole exchange was ridiculous. Some of the kids at those other tables were actually people I'd met that day in my classes, and some of them seemed pretty nice to me. I didn't want to be confined to a certain table or area of the cafeteria based on race, and I didn't care for the way this girl made assumptions. So I challenged the status quo. I became friends with all the tables. Each day I showed up to lunch and got to know a new group of people. I know it drove her insane, and she'd whisper to her other friends when she'd see me talking to someone else she didn't approve of or know. But truthfully, I realized something. Her intolerance was a result of fear and ignorance. She made up assumptions about people because it was easier than getting up from her own table to go meet them. I learned a lot from those new friends I had made that year. It opened my eyes and challenged me to stop making assumptions. Stereotypes are dangerous, and the only way to defeat them is to get to know people for who they are, not what others say.

Come As You Are

Now as I write this, I'm channeling Nirvana and remembering how I walked down the aisle at my second wedding to Harold to that song. I guess I've been breaking rules my whole life. (Funny how I'm writing a book about rules. Ha!) But seriously, when I say "Come As You Are," it means that we need to be welcoming to other women, despite our differences. When we invite a woman to our home for dinner and find out she's a vegetarian or vegan, it means we are respectful of it. We don't avoid getting together with them because they are different. It means we welcome them and offer to learn how to prepare a meal they can eat. Diet is just a tiny part of that, and probably the easiest to understand or talk about. Religion, ethnicity and beliefs are probably the bigger issues we face today, and ones many of us avoid talking about altogether. Once again, if your circle looks and acts just like you, you aren't learning anything. I remember when I first started dating my husband, Harold. I was raised as a Christian, and he was Jewish. I was a little fearful of the differences, especially of what my Christian friends might think or say about it. But ultimately, his faith taught me a lot and only reinforced my love for my religion, while respecting his as well. Our wedding was a beautiful blend of both Christian and Jewish wedding traditions. If I had been close-minded about getting to know him, all because he was different, I would have missed out on the love of my life. The same holds true for the women in our tribes. It's time we stop making assumptions about their beliefs and just say, *"Hey girl! Come on in and sit down. I saved you a seat."* You're not saying, *"I condone your beliefs,"* or *"I approve of your life's choices."* It just means, *"I accept you for who you are."*

When a fellow sister opens up and shares something about herself with you, it's not our job to judge it or offer a differing opinion. For example, if a new sister says, *"I'm an atheist because of something tragic that happened in my church years ago,"* that's not a cue for us to whip out our Bibles and start dragging her back to church. It means holding space for her and saying, *"I am so sorry for whatever you went through. I'm here for you if you ever want to talk."* That's our job as sisters. We don't save them or rescue them. We don't judge them for where they might be right now. We just accept them. I know. I can hear my Southern sisters now, ready to unleash all sorts of scripture on me and tell me why we are supposed to act differently. Save it. I was raised in the church, and I know all about it. I can spew verses all over them, too, but it won't reach them if they don't feel accepted and loved. Do that first. Love them. Welcome them. Encourage them to be authentic and you be authentic, too. If they have questions about the Bible, you'll be the first they'll ask if you're respectful when they tell you their secrets. I know as Christians, we are often called to "share the gospel." But as sisters, I challenge you to build that friendship first. You can't go wrong with love as a strategy. Besides, if you are a Christian, you are called to *be the church* and love how Jesus loved. No judgment. No strings. Live your life in such a way that your atheist friends *want* to know more. Actions speak louder than words, always.

Avoid the Bermuda Triangle

I do a lot of workshops on social media and visibility. I share the best ways to reach your target audience and how to find those ideal clients for your business. I teach on showing up authentically and sharing your mission and vision with your potential clients daily. I also talk a lot about what not to do. One of those things is avoiding the *Bermuda Triangle of Social Media,* which means avoiding three topics in social media that could alienate, offend or anger your followers, which is covered in my book, *The Savvy Girl Media's Guide to Branding.* I remember as a child being fascinated with the Bermuda Triangle. I watched numerous documentaries about planes that would fly over the area, never to be seen again. Hundreds of boats disappeared, and it's always been known as *this black hole to avoid at all costs.* I've heard several theories about what makes it so perilous, but the one that makes the most sense is that there is some sort of magnetic pull or force that disables or counteracts the machinery, electronics or whatever is controlling these planes and boats, ultimately causing them to crash or capsize.

Bermuda Triangle Topic 1: Religion

I think we can equate two particular topics as part of the *Bermuda Triangle of Sisterhood*. Once you go there, you never come back. The first one is religion. It's certainly okay to share that you're a Christian, or you're Jewish, or Muslim, etc. The danger comes when it becomes a focal point of an event or meeting. For example, sharing in a room of 30 women that you believe *"Jewish people are the chosen ones and all Christians are wrong,"* probably isn't going to strengthen relationships. In fact, you probably just ruined a few, not to mention your professional reputation. I highly recommend the sisterhood be a bridge, a place where all are welcome and no one is excluded. Avoid prayers before meals when the group is together. Don't post scripture in social media groups, and don't allow those conversations to take place at the events. If two sisters go to lunch and want to discuss religion, I certainly cannot control that, but I have seen feelings hurt and women who stopped attending following similar conversations, often where one sister felt she was simply "helping" the other by sharing her beliefs. Our personal views and beliefs are a part of who we are, often imprinted upon us as young children. Sometimes we don't even realize how passionate we are about them until someone challenges us. That's why we have to tread lightly when forming friendships, always remembering that we have no idea how someone was raised or what they truly believe. It's okay to ask questions, but be respectful. I'll never forget receiving a call from a new sister who had coffee with a fellow sister that same day, and somehow the topic of religion was discussed. This newer sister was Jewish and mentioned that when the other sister asked her what church she regularly attended. Then she went on to question why she didn't believe Jesus was the Messiah and told her she could end up in hell for eternity if she didn't get *saved* and change her ways. Needless to say, this new sister was discouraged and in tears, though I assured her it wouldn't happen again and not to leave the group over this person's irresponsible actions. I then reminded her that Jesus was Jewish, and that the Bible was pretty clear that God loved the Jewish people and even called them *chosen*, and to never be ashamed of her religion or beliefs. This sister is still a member of my group today, though the sister who made those irresponsible remarks is no longer active in the group.

Bermuda Triangle Topic 2: Politics

The second part of the Bermuda Triangle is politics. I live in a suburb outside of Dallas, Texas. The political climate here is often volatile, and I avoid engaging in that world if at all possible. I remember the night before my women's brunch in 2016, which happened to be Election Night, when Donald Trump became President. Regardless of who I voted for, I was worried about our brunch the following day. The election was already pretty divisive, and sadly, I knew the results wouldn't alleviate the division. When I showed up to the brunch the next morning, you could cut the tension in that room with a knife. Half the group was elated, and could hardly contain themselves, high-fiving each other on the way in, all smiles. The other half of the group was a split between sadness and anger. Two of the women had been in tears just moments before walking into the restaurant. I also had several women register and pay for the event and not show up at all. The emotions were running high for everyone that day, and I had to open the meeting with a powerful message to get us on track for a great meeting. I talked about the election being an external event with internal consequences. But I also shared that we are all leaders of some kind, whether we are leading our groups, our jobs, or our families, and how we choose to react to this election and its results would ultimately be a reflection of who we are, good or bad. I challenged every woman in attendance to forget about whether or not their candidate won or lost and, truly focus on the fact that they had to move on with relationships and friendships, even with those on the other side of the vote. It was the first time my voice trembled when speaking to my own tribe, purely because I knew the weight of the situation. I hate talking about politics and avoid it all costs, except with my husband. He's a "safe" person to discuss it with, but I still don't get too involved or passionate about them because my mission has nothing to do with it. I am not called to preach on religion or educate on politics. I'm here to heal hearts and connect women. My mission is crystal clear and getting political only blurs it and derails me. At times during heated elections, I cringe as I log into social media platforms. I see so many of my sisters engaging in damaging conversations or posting hurtful things. Truthfully, that's why I'm writing this book, or at least one of the many reasons. It's time we re-learn the rules. We need to stop offending our friends in the name of our beliefs.

Politics are already incredibly divisive; we shouldn't make it worse by participating in the rhetoric. Regardless of who you voted for, you should be more interested in the feelings of your friends. The issues from abortion to human rights and beyond all affect us each differently. If you were raised in an abusive household, that affects how you see everything. If you had a teenage sister who became a young mom, your views on abortion might be strong one way or the other. Try to set aside your own personal beliefs to realize our relationships are only as strong as our commitment to accept and respect each other. When I say that politics is part of the Bermuda Triangle, it means avoid it like the plague if you want to be a good Sister. If you have a friend running for office, great! Like their posts and support them. But don't bash another candidate. Don't get caught up in the internet hate wars or engage in arguments. All that does is suck you dry and alienate you from people who believe differently than you. I was recently at a women's networking group, when a speaker went rogue and started talking about religion and politics. It was so uncomfortable, and half the room didn't know how to respond. I lost respect for the speaker and questioned the discernment of the leaders of that group. This wasn't a Christian group, and it certainly wasn't a political group. Why was this being allowed or encouraged? I never went back. Don't assume everyone believes the same as you because they probably don't.

Again, just avoid these divisive topics and focus on forming relationships. It's a lot easier to laugh with your best friend if you have differing views than it is to talk about them over your first coffee meeting together.

When I speak on social media rules and best practices, the third piece of the Bermuda Triangle is sex. This isn't truly a big deal when it comes to the sisterhood, so that's why we really only focus on politics and religion. It was worth mentioning, though. If you're new to a tribe, discussing your sexual life and preferences could prove problematic. You never know what someone has been through or is going through currently, so keep that in mind.

RULE FOUR
CREATE REAL CONNECTIONS

"If only you could sense how important you are to the lives of those you meet; how important you can be to people you may never even dream of. There is something of yourself that you leave at every meeting with another person."

~Fred Rogers

So far I've been laying out the foundation of creating a thriving sisterhood from being absolutely authentic to cheering on other women and being inclusive. These are all imperative pieces of the tribe, but none of it will matter if you can't form true connections with your sisters. When I use the word 'connection,' it's more about breaking through layers and finding a connection to another woman. It's not just sitting with someone at an event and saying, *"These are my new friends!"* That can certainly be a true statement, but we have to dig deeper. It means leaving that event and reaching out to two or three of those women at your table and getting to know them better. What do they love to do on vacation? What's their favorite food? Why do they own a ferret instead of a dog? Why is their nickname *"Betty Spaghetti?"* Being a friend is a responsibility. Saying you have lots of friends may be true, but do you actually spend time with them? I have some friends that I haven't seen or spoken to in years, and yet I still call them friends. But if I had a flat tire on the highway, would they be the first to call? Probably not. Not everyone is your best friend. And that's okay. In fact, I would challenge you to create a drawing of circles to truly identify who you have in your friendship circles.

Far Outer Layer: Acquaintances

The far outer layer of your friends circle are the people you don't really know. Maybe you've met them once or you're connected on social media and never met in person. You don't really know much about them, but they seem friendly. These generally aren't people you'd invite to your home for the holidays, but they could eventually become a closer friend with time or experience. Your acquaintances shouldn't dictate your decisions or warrant change in your life. If someone in this circle told you, *"You should quit that side hustle if you're not making enough money,"* I'd tell you to take it with a grain of salt. They don't know you well enough to care about you or your decisions, so proceed with caution. If someone falls into this category, but you genuinely feel a connection to them, explore it to see if there's more there. Grab lunch or coffee and get to know them better. Sometimes social media gives us a false sense of someone's personality or life, and only a real live conversation can clarify that for us.

Outer Layer: Frenemies

The outer layer is comprised of your frenemies. If you've never heard this term before, it's basically a friend who is secretly an enemy. It's unfortunate that this group of people have to be a part of your circle, but it's necessary. These are really your enemies who parade around as friends. You know firsthand they are gossipers or haters, and you've seen them burn you or your friends in the past. These are the ones who show up to events and never really connect with anyone on a deeper level, and then bad-mouth the group or event to others because they see there's magic happening - and they don't like it. Typically this person is acting sheerly out of jealousy or envy and cannot make true connections until they come to terms with their inner demons. I once would have told you to kick these people out of your circle, but it's just not realistic. Unfortunately, it creates more drama than it's worth, and I find it's just best to let them show themselves out over time. I have learned from experience the havoc it can wreak when you try to remove these people from your circle, which is why I just recommend you restrict them on social media, unfollow them and limit interaction with them. Eventually, you hope, they will move on and sink their teeth into someone else.

Inner Layer One: Fun Friends

The next layer of your friends circle is likely made up of those you've met in person a few times and have enjoyed some fun events sitting next to them or talking with them. You could hang out with them and have a great time, but you don't really know anything about them. The conversation likely never went beyond the weather or occupations. You couldn't name their children or grandchildren to save your life, and you may not even know what they do for a living. They may have even dominated the conversation, and you left feeling like you never got a word in edgewise. They seem friendly and full of life, but you'd have to spend more time with them to really feel like you could trust them with your secrets. Again, if you feel inclined, reach out to them and meet them one-on-one for a coffee or lunch and explore the friendship. Sometimes these friends can evolve into closer friends with time.

Inner Layer Two: Professional Friends

These are the peeps in your circle who you've connected with on a professional level, either because you have worked together or they were a client of yours, or vice versa. You likely have spent some time together and know quite a bit about them. You trust their advice and expertise, and your meetings are always productive or inspiring. You wouldn't hesitate to refer friends or family to them, and you highly respect them. You may not ever approach sensitive or personal subjects, so as to keep the relationship professional in nature. Over time, though, these people may easily develop into good friends.

Innermost Layer: Good Friends

This is often where your circle starts to get smaller and smaller. Many women I know only have a handful of good friends. Before I created The Every Heart Project, I only had about two women I could name in this category. But this is the ultimate place where you should want to funnel the sweetest and most inspiring women you know. The only way to do that? Real connection. Meet them for lunch, invite them over for dinner, do a double date. It takes time and effort to build those relationships, and they don't happen by accident. It's intentional. Your good friends are the ones who know a lot about you and accept you for who you are. They feel bad if they forget your birthday, and they reach out when they notice you've been MIA on social media lately. They are always in your corner. and they defend you when others talk badly behind your back. Your goal is to keep growing this layer, constantly deepening those connections and strengthening those relationships.

The Bullseye: Best Friends

The center of the circle of friends is one of the most important, for a variety of reasons. As women, we have an innate need to feel like someone "gets" us or understands us. We need that connection that can only be found with best friends. It means you can tell them your deepest, darkest secrets, and they would never tell a soul. These are the ones who will gladly show up if you have a flat tire and will bring you chocolate and wine after the whole traumatic ordeal. They have your back in all situations and would leave a group if they felt it betrayed you in any way.

You can travel with them, take road trips, share holidays, and even tolerate their kids and family. They are the first ones you call when you've had a bad day or if you have amazing news. They share in your wins and offer a shoulder when you lose.

Now, I know this is going to make your eyebrows raise a bit, but be careful before placing the 'best friend' stamp on a friend. Make sure they really care about you and your success, and pay attention to the signs. If they constantly cancel on you, or you catch them in little lies, they may not be as loyal as you may think. You might have assumed they are your bestie, and they may have slotted you into the frenemy category. I know it's a bit discouraging to think you have to constantly be watching and listening for signs, but I just want to emphasize that this layer of friendship is the closest to your heart and has the most access to you. Always make sure you've categorized it correctly before baring your soul. I learned this one the hard way. There was a woman in my circle who I lovingly called my 'bestie' and told her absolutely everything. We were inseparable and talked almost daily. Then one day I found out she was telling everything I said to another friend and even spreading some untrue things as well within our circle of friends. I have since 'removed' her from this layer and moved her to the frenemy group. These are the people we need to limit interaction with, and I'm extremely careful what I share with her now because of her past behaviors. I still care for her, which is why I didn't end our friendship. I also recognize that her reasoning for sharing has more to do with her own need to be 'in the know' and less to do with me. Either way, she's not a best friend.

Here's the beauty of the friends circle: we need all of these in the circle. Your sisterhood or Tribe should represent all of these layers, even the frenemies. In order to function as a true sisterhood, all of the layers work together to form a cohesive, yet diverse tribe. You can't build a huge tribe of best friends. It just won't happen. But within the sisterhood, each sister will start to find their best friends and their good friends, and everything in between. It's okay to know someone new is still an acquaintance, and it takes time and intentional effort to establish those connections to elevate the friendship into something deeper. And that's completely natural.

Not everyone deserves a seat at your table. Yes, in the first rule, I talked about how there are plenty of seats at the table. But this is your personal table. Think of Thanksgiving when you where a kid, and there was always a kids' table. When you hit a certain age and maturity, you were permitted to join the grown-ups. The same is true in your sisterhood. It's okay to meet someone new and not feel they fit in with you. Get to know them and see if your outlook changes. It might or it might not. We aren't going to click with everyone we meet. We aren't meant to, and that's just the way life is sometimes. But everyone we meet can teach us something, if we just look for it. We all have something in common with another woman, even if it's something small. Our job as sisters isn't to find the differences; it's to find the commonalities. Look at it as a scavenger hunt. Keep on asking questions until you find something that unites you. It might take ten minutes, or it might take ten months. Don't stress if it doesn't unfold into a gorgeous friendship. Life is funny that way. I think of when my daughter, Ariana, was a little girl. I became friends with another mom at the school, someone with whom I felt an instant connection. She also had a daughter the same age. I was so excited! "Let's have a playdate!" I exclaimed, and proceeded to be completely devastated when the girls hated each other. Well, I guess hate is a strong word. But they didn't like each other at all. So if we wanted to be friends as moms, it might not be around the premise of our daughters being best friends. We can't force connections. It's called chemistry, and it either happens or it doesn't.

Don't Give Up

When you don't get along with some of the women in your tribe, it doesn't mean you need to leave the tribe. It simply means you haven't identified your friends funnel yet. Give it time. Meet more of them for coffee or lunch and start to identify who you click with and who you just don't click with at all. If you haven't found a best friend in the group yet, bring one in! I can't stress this enough! Perhaps your bestie is supposed to be a part of my good friend group or a part of someone else's professional friends group. We can all learn from each other on some level. Remember, don't be stingy with your tribe or your friends! If you love the group, but haven't really connected with anyone yet on a deeper level, you have work to do. Don't give up before discovering the gold. The best sisterhoods are the ones that have figured out how to teach their members to cultivate relationships. The friendship funnel is always changing, and friends will move from acquaintances to frenemies to good friends and so on. That's the natural way of relationships. The best way to manage it is to let go of your expectations. Allow relationships to naturally grow or grow apart. Don't force it, and watch for the lessons you will learn.

Be a Secret-Keeper

One of the hardest lessons I ever learned was about keeping secrets. I love to tell stories, and sometimes telling someone else's secret feels like a forbidden story you shouldn't tell. And that's because it should be forbidden. I betrayed the trust of someone and quickly realized that sharing that secret only hurt our friendship and my reputation. Yes, I was young, but it's no excuse. Behavior isn't less wrong depending on age, unless you're my mother-in-law, who is a five-time cancer survivor and pretty much allowed to say and do anything at the age of 75. Lord help me if Shelley ever reads this. Love you, Mom! Anyway, that was a mistake I only made once. Never again. To this day, if someone says to me, *"I have a secret, but you can't tell anyone,"* I reflect back on that moment in my twenties when I learned that hard lesson. I keep those secrets now. To the death! No one will ever know, and that's imperative in building your reputation as a sister who can be trusted. Keep those secrets and never betray your fellow sister.

RULE FIVE
CHECK YOUR EGO AT THE DOOR

"Your ego reacts with emotion and your heart responds with love. Results depend on which one you choose."

~Roxana Jones

I remember back in 2014 when I first started my women's group. I took over an existing chapter of a national women's organization, where the ladies had only been meeting once per month at night, only about 8-10 women showing up each month. I had this crazy idea of doing a "Power Brunch" during the workday, primarily for women who owned their own business or had flexible schedules to meet for lunch during the day. The premise of the brunch was to share a challenge they were facing in their business and ask the other ladies for assistance or advice. The problem was that it turned into a two-hour, nonstop sales pitch-a-thon. One by one, the women would stand up, state their name and business name, and then their "challenge" they would share would essentially be *"I need more clients."* I kept gently steering the attendees back to the purpose of the brunch, reminding them of the vision. After a few months of realizing it just wasn't working, I decided to address the elephant in the room. My brunch had already grown from 8 to 20 women in a few short months, as the word began to get out about this awesome format. Apparently no one else had thought of this idea before, or at least not consistently. When introducing myself at the next brunch, I used a phrase that seemed to shock everyone a bit, and even made a few chuckle. I told the women, *"Check your ego at the door."* I went on to add, "This brunch is not about asking for sales or sharing your latest product or service. We are cultivating relationships, and that requires vulnerability and honesty. Take this opportunity to truly share a challenge you are facing and allow these brilliant women to selflessly help you. We should be a community of women helping each other. That's the purpose for today's brunch. Everyone understand?" I even went as far as to direct them to look at the door and remind them that is where we leave our egos when we arrive each and every month.

The tone of that brunch changed. The women opened up, dropped their masks, and magic happened in that restaurant that day. True friendships began to form with many of the women, and watching it all unfold truly touched my heart and confirmed my mission. Yes, building relationships can be hard for many women to do, especially if they've been burned in the past. We tend to carry our old hurts and bruises as badges of honor, citing them as the reason we never let our guard down or get close to another woman again. I get it. I really do. I've been burned in the past as well. Heck, I've been burned this week alone! Relationships can get messy, and that's simply a part of life. But the magic can't happen until you open up and be vulnerable. The brunch would be just like every other networking event if I hadn't challenged the status quo and encouraged these women to be different. I'm so glad I took that leap and risked it. It was so worth it.

How Can You Serve Your Sister?

The easiest way to create an environment of giving is to focus on service. When a new woman shows up for a brunch meeting, I still use that *"check your ego at the door"* phrase, and I add, *"we are here to serve each other."* You may have an incredible product or service, but that's not how you pitch it. If you are a real estate agent, and someone says, *"I'm thinking about putting my house on the market and I have some questions,"* the spirit of service is more about giving advice without expectation of getting the listing. This can be hard, and not only for real estate agents. We spend so much time marketing our businesses and trying to find those ideal clients, and then we find a potential one right there in front of us, basically screaming, *"I'm your absolute perfect client!"* But that's where we fail. They aren't ready to be your client yet. They are testing the waters to see if you can be trusted. With the wrong reaction, your chance is shot. They will close back up and you'll never get the client. Always give without expectation, and you'll never be disappointed. Instead of trying to convert them to clients, ask yourself, *"How can I serve them in a way that would make them trust me and come back to me in the future?"* Think about the last time you bought a new car. Did you really love that pushy salesperson, or did you appreciate the laid-back one who gave you some space? My husband and I bought a new car together last summer, and it was the first time we felt as though the salesperson was brutally honest and didn't just lie to make the sale. He was genuine and human, and we both trusted him. It made our car buying experience fun and pleasant, which made all the difference. People don't want to feel pressured to buy, so don't do that, especially to your sisters. Otherwise you miss the opportunity to build a friendship.

Communication Care

Following our women's brunches and evening events, I often hear about sisters being solicited for business by a fellow sister, unexpectedly. Typically, one sister might share a challenge during the brunch and ask for advice. Another sister sitting nearby will take note of said challenge, and follow-up with that sister a few days later to pitch her product or service. This is absolutely the opposite of what we need to be doing to cultivate relationships. Once again, how can you serve them without selling them? With every email, phone call and private message you send, you are solidifying your reputation. Do you want to be known as that person who has no regard for building the relationship and only cares about sales or referrals? My assumption is that is not what you truly want, but perhaps this is what you've been taught or learned. If you want to be the sister others can trust, and eventually who they come to for advice or to get pricing on your services, you have to unlearn those old behaviors. No one wants to be sold, especially by someone they thought cared about them as a friend or sister. We do business with people we know, like and trust. You can't skip the steps. Get to know your sisters first, so they can get to know you and start to like you. Trust is earned. Take extra care when you send a new sister an email or private message. Make sure you are doing so with pure motives. Your reputation is always on the line.

Sisters Protect Their Sisters

Also remember that if a sister learns you are a predatory salesperson, she will likely warn other sisters to protect them. This kind of news spreads quickly, so tread lightly. Unfortunately, I've seen this happen so often in our circle, and it typically alienates friendships and has even prevented potential new members from joining our group after an incident. Last year, following our third annual women's retreat, I started to receive numerous concerns from members of our group about one of the retreat attendees messaging them to pitch her product. It wasn't very subtle either, as she was simply doing that whole 'copy and paste' thing with all the emojis, and blasting it out to her entire friends list. The problem was that she wasn't even making an attempt to get to know them first or meet for coffee to nurture the relationship. In fact, there was no offer of an in-person meeting at all! Her entire message was something like, *"Hey girl! I have this fabulous new product and I'd love to send you a free sample. No obligation to buy! Send me your address if you're interested!"* It sounds harmless, but it's not done from a pure motive. Furthermore, it's tied to a network marketing group, which I'll explore more about later. I probably received 10 complaints about this one person, which prompted me to reach out to her in a friendly, diplomatic way, in an attempt to gently remind her that this type of behavior could be damaging her reputation and her friendships with the sisters. She, of course, denied she was doing anything wrong, and proceeded to cancel her reservation for the following year's retreat. She also unfriended some of the sisters who initially raised concerns. Overall, I'm slightly relieved she removed herself from the group, because the next retreat would have been very awkward after her behavior. I actually feel sorry for her, because she will likely reflect back upon her actions and realize she could have behaved differently.

Criticism is Deadly

First of all, constructive criticism in many situations can be helpful and appreciated. With that being said, most criticism is delivered poorly and is often ineffective. If you witness a sister delivering an elevator pitch at a networking event you're both attending, and she says all the wrong things and starts beating herself up, that's not the perfect time to deliver criticism. Offer to meet with her one-on-one to practice with her, or give her some positive feedback. Knowing when to keep things positive is probably the most important aspect here. If she's already beating herself up, which we as women tend to be phenomenal at doing, skip the chance to add to her pity party. Sometimes being a great sister means supporting them even when they're doing a mediocre job at something. Always ask yourself, *"Is it worth me jeopardizing my friendship to share my knowledge and expertise with her?"* My guess is that the answer is usually no in that scenario. Don't get me wrong. There is a right way to gently guide a sister who needs some help, but they have to be receptive and willing to receive it. Many of them just aren't ready yet. Always avoid criticizing another sister in public or in front of others. This will permanently taint your relationship, as well as your reputation. And never talk badly of other sisters when they're not in the room. Gossip is a poison that spreads like a wildfire throughout women's groups everywhere and creates division and conflict. Avoid it like the plague and encourage others not to engage in it either. Once it starts, it often can't stop until it destroys everything.

Don't be a KIA

First of all, a KIA is a know-it-all. No, I'm not talking about a foreign car here, (although I'm sure I could come up with some analogies to match it as well. I do love a good challenge.) I remember meeting a woman in a networking group many years ago. I had quoted something from a book as part of a conversation, and she immediately stopped me to correct my quote, as I had left out one word. She then proceeded to tell me she had an MBA and was a proud member of MENSA. I made a mental note to never hang out with her again. That very first interaction completely turned me off and prevented me from wanting to form a relationship with her. She may be a loving person with lots of amazing friends, but someone who knows everything can be downright annoying. They often interrupt others sharing a story to interject facts or corrections. They may question everything you say and challenge you repeatedly. Over time, these types of people become known as hecklers or haters, and may even find themselves not invited to other events because of past behaviors. If you tend to be a KIA, my advice to you would be to learn to listen. Shut up when you really want to correct someone's story or grammar, and learn to nod your head and smile. No one cares if you know everything, unless you're auditioning for a trivia game show. Save your knowledge for your blog or YouTube channel. Otherwise you will be damaging your reputation and risking your relationships with other sisters.

The Platinum Rule

We all know the Golden Rule, right?

"Treat others as you would like to be treated."

Have I triggered you back to your kindergarten memories with your pigtails and juice boxes yet? We all learned this rule at an early age, and it was drilled into us like the Pledge of Allegiance. The premise is that you treat others exactly how *you* would wish to be treated. Seems pretty fair. But there's a new rule in town, and one that is probably better and more applicable in the sisterhood. It's called the Platinum Rule, and it states, *"Treat others as THEY would like to be treated."* So no longer do you care about how you would want to be treated. You are to, once again, form relationships with others first so you can know their preferences. If you never take the time to recognize that this one sister prefers email over text, and how this other sister lost two loved ones last year and struggles with depression, then you're missing the big stuff. Think about personality types, love languages, and communication styles. We are all different. Some may be more blunt and to the point in their communication whereas others may be quite timid. Some may be quite emotional, and others very stoic. Until you take the time to cultivate the relationships, you won't be able to know how they wish to be treated. Friendships take time to build. Do the work. It's definitely worth it.

Ego Vs. Heart

The ego isn't necessarily a bad thing at all. Our egos protect us and help us find confidence when we need it. For many, tapping into that happened later in life, especially if we spent many years building a family and nurturing others. Ego usually takes a back seat for young moms and wives, though men are encouraged to develop it at a young age. With many of our Heart Sisters, they finally began to tap into their egos following something difficult, such as the loss of a marriage, a death in the family, a job layoff or even their kids leaving home. They suddenly find themselves in a situation where they need to show strength and gumption, and the ego can prove instrumental and imperative. Our hearts are totally different but can work in harmony with our egos if we understand each one's purpose. When forming relationships with our sisters, our egos will whisper things like, *"You're better than her,"* or *"Don't give her all of your knowledge for free!"* when you may be offering advice in an effort to be of service. Your heart exists to connect and will whisper things like, *"She needs love,"* or *"Shower her with compliments - she needs them."* Your heart is focused on developing a deeper connection with those you meet. But your heart cannot always be trusted. If you do not also use your brain and your ego, you may be too trusting of those who will take advantage of you or who have ulterior motives. I often say The Every Heart Project is a heart-led organization, but that doesn't mean we don't use our heads as well. Yes, the heart can deceive you, but learning to listen to each of the messages from the heart, ego, brain and even gut instincts will serve you as you navigate these relationships.

RULE SIX
SHOW UP

"Show up in every single moment like you are meant to be there."

~Marie Forleo

If any of my Heart Sisters are reading this book, they probably know I could write an entire book on showing up. I've always been quite vocal about this topic, and it all started when I first launched my women's group back in 2014. My very first event was planned, and I had booked the private room at the restaurant and planned the agenda. I had more than 25 women who signed up to attend, and I was so freaking excited I could hardly wait. Upon arrival to the restaurant, I set up my welcome sign and prepared the room for 25 women. An hour later, only three women had shown up, and the program was disjointed since the activities planned were meant for a larger group. I gave as much value to those attending as possible, but I left feeling incredibly defeated and discouraged. I came home in tears, relaying to my husband the lack of attendance and my incredible frustration. He tried to soothe me, reminding me that I was new to the role, and not to stress about the numbers in attendance right away. *"You have to start somewhere,"* he wisely stated. He was right. I knew that. But it didn't change the fact that we had a problem. Women were signing up for events, clicking "yes" and then never showing up.

This issue frustrated me so much I ended up writing an article about it that went viral. One day, following an event where more than 20 women hadn't shown up, I took to my computer and started to draft an article on the social media platform LinkedIn. It was titled, *"Why Women Don't Show Up, and Then Feel Bad About It."* I started writing it from a place of disappointment, but as the words flowed out of my head and onto the screen, the words transformed into something quite beautiful. I was sympathizing with them, citing reasons and offering real world advice on how to stop falling into that guilt trap. At the time, most of my articles had only gained the attention of a handful of people, so I didn't really expect what happened next.

That article was written during the week, and I didn't log back into the site again for several days. That following Sunday morning, I went to grab my phone from the charger and quickly skim my emails for important messages. I had about fifty emails from LinkedIn. *"Oh crap,"* I said out loud, to which my husband replied, *"What's up?"* I sat down on the edge of the bed to open LinkedIn and see what was possibly going on. *"I may have been hacked or something."* When I opened LinkedIn, I had more than 500 notifications, all related to my article on not showing up. I also had messages from women all over the world, thanking me for writing it! They were actually thanking me for speaking up about them not showing up! I couldn't believe it. I opened the article statistics and saw my article had already reached more than 3000 people, and had hundreds of likes, comments and shares. I was so humbled, and instantly felt gratitude for social media platforms. What a wonderful world in which we live where we can simply write something and post it and reach thousands of other people. I attempted to respond to each and every comment, which I knew would take hours. I did it anyway. And I vowed to never forget that feeling of thankfulness. The response to that article was unexpected and appreciated. I ended up writing a follow up piece the next week, more focused on how we turn around this behavior. It didn't have the same reach as the first one, but it still traveled the globe with its message.

Sadly, women not showing up is still a problem today, though I've created some consequences for those who struggle with it. All of my events now require a fee to register, even if it's small. I don't offer refunds or allow tickets to be transferred. Some may view it as a harsh policy, but it's meant to help our women begin to understand why showing up and being reliable is so important. I also lead by example and show them when I sign up to attend an event, I follow through and show up. If you struggle with this, know that you are not alone. So many women, and many in my own group, battle anxiety, depression and other challenges that often manifest in their inability to show up or be dependable. Following a recent event, one sister reached out to me and thanked me for a wonderful night. She admitted she had circled the building twice and debated not coming in, all because of her social anxiety, and finally mustered up the courage to walk in. My heart breaks that so many struggle with this, but I'm so thankful that I'm creating a safe place for them to land. No judgment. No pressure.

Integrity Matters

In the end, all we have is our integrity. When dealing with something difficult or challenging, how we show up and behave truly does matter. Every time we say we will be there and we do not show up, we taint our own reputations just a bit. We all have that friend we secretly know is a little bit flaky. You've invited her to parties, events, your wedding... but seriously, every time we don't show up, we inadvertently say to them, *"I can't be trusted."* Whoa. That's pretty tough. I hear you saying that now, but it's true. Even in a time where everyone is flaky, choose to be different. We are a society of *"maybes,"* and it's hurting us all. One of my friends on Facebook recently posted, *"I'm not going to show up, but keep inviting me."* Umm, no. That's not how this works, sweetie. If you are consistently unavailable or flaky, the invitations will eventually cease. So when someone asks you to attend an event, do not immediately say yes, unless you are certain you can attend and want to. Don't ignore the 'want to' piece either! It matters. At the end of a tough day, the last event you will want to attend is one you've been seriously dreading. When they tell you what the event is all about, pay attention to how the description makes you feel. Do you get all warm and fuzzy inside and instantly know it's an event you will love? Or do you roll your eyes inside your head and secretly prefer a root canal over attending? I'm serious. Pay attention to those feelings. They will ultimately guide you in the hours or minutes just before you're supposed to show up. All of a sudden, you'll feel this overwhelming thought of *"I really don't want to attend this event."* You had that feeling before, but you buried it beneath your choice of pleasing someone else.

Choose Wisely

When someone invites me to an event, there are a few questions I ask myself before I respond. First of all, do I like this person and value them as a friend, trusted partner, referral source, etc? If yes, I move onto the next question. If no, I politely tell them I cannot attend. The second question I ask myself is whether or not this event will be good for my business or result in personal or professional growth. Will I find value in this event? Or will I feel as though I've wasted time or money? The final question I ask myself is more about logistics. How does the time and location fit with my schedule? For example, I host two or more events each month for my women's group, with the evening event usually on a Thursday night. If I'm invited to an event for that Friday morning, I'm likely to turn down that invitation because I'm usually pretty exhausted following the evening event. I already know that waking up early the next morning, getting dressed and driving somewhere for another event isn't going to be appealing to me. Now if I'm over the moon excited about the event, or it's for a dear friend or family member, I'm likely to set aside my own personal preferences and still attend. That's why those questions matter. Ask yourself each of them and pay attention to your answers. I'd rather be known as the person who can't say yes than the one who always says yes but never shows up.

Missed Connections

My women's group hosts a retreat weekend each year, typically in the fall, and I'm currently in the planning stages for our fourth annual retreat. The magic that happens at that event is truly indescribable, and many former attendees still talk about those memories. I remember fondly so many of the moments at the first three retreats, from staying up late playing games to sharing stories by the fire on s'mores night. So many lifelong friendships were made during those weekends, and my prayer is to host this event each and every year to reach more and more women. Last year, we had several members who were unable to commit to attending the retreat. They each had different reasons, and I respect that completely, but one member reached out to me and said she wishes there was a way to form these kinds of connections without staying in a hotel for the weekend. I was caught by surprise by her comment, but I proceeded to share with her that attending the retreat is a choice. It's no different than choosing to take three days off work and go away on vacation. We all make decisions based on priority. If the retreat was a priority, then you'd find a way to attend. If not, you'll find an excuse. But you can't turn down the opportunity to make magical connections and then say we need to manufacture them elsewhere. There's no way to create these kinds of moments in a two hour evening program or a brunch event. It just can't happen. When you fail to show up, you miss out. But you have to own that decision. You can say no all day and boast about it on social media, citing *"self-care"* and *"proud introvert,"* but then whining about what you're missing only negates your decision to say no. Stand by your choice and deal with the consequences.

Show Up for Each Other

Beyond showing up to our women's events each month, I encourage you to show up for each other. This means that when a sister reaches out to you and invites you to lunch or coffee, you say yes and you show up. I'm heartbroken when I receive those phone calls of members who have had several sisters cancel last minute for their scheduled meetings. One woman had driven more than thirty miles before 7 o'clock in the morning to meet another sister, only to get a text fifteen minutes before their proposed meeting time that she wouldn't make it. This jilted sister called me in tears and asked if she was doing something wrong. My wish for women everywhere is that we'd begin to conscientiously make decisions and follow through with them. My prayer is that we stop making last minute decisions that have devastating consequences, all for a little temporary relief. There's a human holding a phone on the other end of that cancelation text you just sent. There's a person sitting inside a coffee shop alone now because you waited until the last minute to cancel, not realizing she showed up an hour early to prepare or had to coordinate childcare to make it all work. We have no idea the turmoil we cause when we don't show up. From leaders and event organizers to sisters and potential referral partners, we are creating a dangerous pattern for everyone else to follow and emulate. It's time to stop.

Self-Care vs. Selfishness

Our society has completely glamourized the term self-care. We've used it to justify our last minute decisions to bail on events, relationships and more. It's no longer just the need to take a few hours to recharge; it's become this inflated feeling of entitlement. For example, I often see these quotes pop up in my social media feeds about *"It's okay to cancel an appointment or take a day off to protect your energy."* I call bullshit. If I only showed up whenever I felt like it, there wouldn't be The Every Heart Project. I remember hosting our brunch one November morning in 2015, just an hour after finding out my husband had been laid off and was en route on a train from downtown. I couldn't cancel the brunch. I remember the following November when my brunch fell the morning after Election Day when President Trump won the election. I really didn't want to show up that morning, but it was even more imperative that I did. How we choose to rise (or not) is what determines how we feel about ourselves and, ultimately, shapes our reputation.

The Guys Don't Struggle With This

I've never once heard my husband say, *"I signed up for this event, but now I don't want to go."* If he bought a ticket, he's in the car and headed there. Why do women struggle, yet the guys never do? I still don't understand this, but I'm bringing it up to challenge us to do better. Sisters, we know women have immense strength and resolve, so why do we cave when it comes to our schedules and sticking with our plans? It's time to stop beating ourselves up and start showing up. I recently challenged myself with attending 10 events in two weeks. They were all over the Dallas/Fort Worth metroplex, which meant a few of them were more than 30 minutes away. I signed up for each of them, paid the fees, and put them on my calendar. I paid attention to the various thoughts that kept creeping up with each of them as it became time to go. I definitely felt the urge to cancel last minute or use the *"I'm not feeling great"* excuse, as so many of my sisters have used when canceling before the evening event or a brunch or workshop. But I chose to keep my promise to myself and show up. I didn't miss one event, and I ended up feeling incredibly thankful I attended all of them. I learned so much from each event and even felt a common message emerge that ended up inspiring me to start this book. I also felt quite proud of myself for following through. Yes, I care about my reputation, but I care more about how I feel about myself and my reputation. I love being the reliable one. I like that my sisters know if I say yes to an event, I'm there on time with a smile to support them. There's power in that. What are you known for?

Showing up is more than just attendance. It's about commitment and follow through. It's about keeping your word and making intentional decisions to accept or decline invitations based on those important questions and not about pleasing others. When we show up, we encourage others to do the same. If everyone else is flaky, be different. You have the power to make the change, so do it.

RULE SEVEN
UPGRADE YOUR BRA

"We attract what we think we deserve."

~Janet Bernstein

You might be standing in the middle of a bookstore, somehow glanced at the table of contents, and quickly flipped to this page out of sheer curiosity for the chapter title. I'm down with that. However you found this book, this information needs to be shared, so pop a squat in the middle of that bookstore and prepare to absorb this information.

Our society is negative.

Our social media feeds are filled with negative posts, devastating information, tragic stories and sadness. It's hard to stay positive at times, surrounded by so much of the opposite. We've also become comfortable with being broke, and sharing it with friends, family and strangers. I see an overwhelming number of posts complaining about the price of things, or how our desire to travel is being squashed by the solemn number in our bank account. When someone posts a picture of their view from their vacation hotel room, overlooking the ocean, I'm shocked to see the initial reactions from friends. There's always one person who immediately writes, *"jealous!"* in the comments. We are not meant to be jealous of another person's success or life. We should simply cheer them on and tell them to enjoy their vacation! That jealous comment may seem trivial, but it speaks volumes.

What does any of this have to do with bras? Stay with me. I'm getting there. I promise.

Last year I enrolled in an online course centered around money mindset and attracting abundance. I began the various modules, one of which was evaluating everything in our lives and categorizing them into various levels, such as economy, business class and first class. One of the things I noticed was that my bras fell into the economy category, as they were no longer well-fitting, and I knew I needed to upgrade. I remember having lunch with a fellow sister and confessing this to her, and she immediately quipped back, *"Girl, bras are expensive. I hold onto mine until they fall apart."* I reflected on her words, and quickly realized that our bras are representative of what we feel we deserve in life. This fellow sister was unhappy in her job, frustrated with her marriage, and the bra was just icing on the cake. When we don't place importance on the things in our lives that truly affect us on a daily basis, such as our jobs, our marriages and our bras, we are subconsciously telling the Universe (or God or whomever you pray to) that we aren't worth it. We are sending the subtle message that we don't deserve more.

Our chest is the part of our body that protects the heart. Below it, all of our precious organs that control our breathing, digestion, and everything else we need to function in this world. Now think about the bra for a minute. It's basically a tool that supports us and protects us. Wearing an ill-fitting bra can be uncomfortable and distract us from an otherwise amazing day. If you've ever been in the middle of an event and felt the underwire pop out of the seam and stab you in the side, you know exactly what I'm talking about. It's time we start taking pride in our undergarments and feeling great about it. Furthermore, we need to encourage our fellow sisters to upgrade their own bras, and their lives. Yes, I'm using the bra analogy because it's funny, but it's a metaphor for everything in your life.

Marriage

If your marriage sucks, ask yourself why. Does it need help in the form of counseling, or do you need to upgrade your partner? When you meet with a sister who constantly complains about her husband, perhaps after the fifth time, you gently suggest she make some tough decisions. I'm not suggesting all of our unhappy sisters go out and file for divorce next week. But if you've been unhappy for a long time and there are no solutions being presented by you or your spouse to make improvements or changes, it might be time to let go. I made that incredibly tough decision many years ago, and it ended up being the best thing for me. We attract what we think we deserve. If you do not have a partner who truly supports you or uplifts you, it's because you've allowed that behavior to endure. If your husband cheats on you, do you simply smile and say, *"That's just how he is"*? Probably not. So why do we not speak up when they display other behaviors that upset us or disappoint us? What we tolerate will always continue.

Career

Our jobs and careers are so integral to our happiness, as we spend so much time at places of employment or working in our businesses. When our careers aren't flourishing, we feel it with every fiber of our being. It haunts us at night, it creeps up on Sunday evening before we start preparing for the work week again, as the dread of returning to a job we hate seeps in again. So many people endure years and years at jobs they don't love or even like. Some even accept abuse or hostile work environments, all because it "pays the bills." If this sounds like you, I'm going to challenge you to make a change. There are so many opportunities out there to make income, and you do not have to suffer in silence in a job you hate, unless you want to. It really is a choice we make. As someone who was let go from a cushy corporate job a few years ago, I can tell you I made the choice to never return to that environment. I decided I wanted something better. I set my own hours, and I have to seek out alternatives to health insurance and other benefits no longer available outside the corporate world, but I'm in charge. Are there crappy months and times I question my own sanity? Heck yeah! But I'm happy. And I'm thankful. Life is way too short to hate our jobs. Do yourself a favor and make a goal of getting out of a job you hate, if this applies to you. You are worth it. Dust off your resume and make a list of ideal jobs. Visualize the perfect job for you, and start working toward making it a reality.

Friendships

I've given you a lot of tools on how to build great relationships with your sisters. I've laid out the rules for being a better sister and truly living with integrity and authenticity in all that you do. With that being said, sometimes we have to upgrade the friends we've had forever. You've been there. You are out to lunch with a long-time friend, and suddenly you realize that the two of you have grown apart in various ways. She's now critical and prone to gossip about friends you both used to know. She's in an unhappy marriage, and you personally feel drained every time she talks about it. She is always broke but refuses to get a job or do anything to change it. She makes fun of the server for forgetting the ranch on the side. Whatever happens during that lunch, you have an epiphany that this friend is no longer someone you want to be intimately connected to. We've all heard the saying that we become like the five people we spend the most time with, and that scares the shit out of you. That's a sign, my friend. It's okay if you distance yourself from that friend for a while and take an upgrade. Find a sister in your life who is where you want to be, achieving what you want to achieve. Make a lunch date with her. Over time, upgrade your friends and surround yourself with higher reaching sisters. Soon you'll be reaching higher levels as well.

We need to be constantly encouraging our sisters, as well as ourselves, to aim for more and stop apologizing for wanting to improve. We are worth it, ladies. I'm worth it. You're worth it. We are meant to have an abundant life, if only we open our eyes and claim it. If a fellow sister is settling for less and boasting about the struggle, grab her hand and remind her she is worth more. Order the more expensive tequila in your margarita at girls' night. Insist on that decadent dessert that makes you feel like a million bucks. Buy that new leather wallet you've been drooling over at the mall if you want it. Send a message that you're ready for a first class life, and go out and get it!

RULE EIGHT
PUT YOUR BUSINESS SECOND (OR THIRD)

"Priorities lead to prosperity."

~Michelle Singletary

This chapter is probably the one that will piss off the most people, and I'm okay with that. Truthfully, it's how I built a tribe that's different from all the others. When it comes to creating a thriving sisterhood, it's all about relationships. Sometimes we fail to remember that and fall back into our selfish ways. We all do it. The key is to self-correct and come back around to the mission. Your business (or mine for that matter) isn't so important that it's worth risking friendships for nor is it our only purpose in this world. You may be the most important woman in the world, running a business saving lives or making real change in the world. None of it will compare to the rewards of a thriving sisterhood of which you feel as though you are an integral part of both creating and sustaining. I guarantee you that no one confesses in their final moments that they wish they'd worked harder or achieved more. They don't long for more hours to sit behind a desk or sell another product. The regrets most often heard are a result of failed friendships, broken families and lost loves. We tend to struggle the most with forgiveness, both asking for it and doling it out after a disagreement or miscommunication. Our egos often prevent us from the desire to repair a relationship, though in the end we realize it's what mattered most all along.

It's Not All About You

Regardless of how we may feel at times, especially when we are caught up in the endless drama of finding new clients or prospects, it's not all about us. When we meet people, if we can only talk nonstop about our businesses, they will tune out pretty quickly. I always make it a habit to just keep asking questions, and I rarely bring up my business until asked. This works beautifully. In fact, if someone asks me more about my business, sometimes I'll say, *"This event is all about celebrating*

_____, *so how about we take some time to get together and I can tell you more."* Believe it or not, this works. Even if someone asks you about your business, it isn't a green light to verbally pitch them or sell your newest product or service. Usually they are only being polite, and once you shift into high sales mode, you've lost the chance to build that relationship. Try to focus on getting to know the other person, especially if it's the first time you've met them. Some of the women in my group tell me their biggest pet peeve is when someone they thought was genuinely trying to become their friend only invites them to coffee to pitch them a product. Don't be that person. Once you do that, you will develop a reputation for being that person who doesn't truly care about anyone but themselves. This can be a challenging thing to overcome, and I've seen it truly hinder the growth of some incredible budding friendships.

Be a Resource

There's a popular graphic that circulates on social media from time to time, and it says, *"Be a resource, not a sales pitch."* I love this quote because it's a good reminder for our business-minded women in the tribe to distinguish themselves from their competition. If you are the most knowledgeable realtor in the area, it's because you offer advice and expertise to others, even if they aren't your clients yet. You give more than you take. When I get asked to meet for coffee or lunch, I sort of expect people to ask me for advice on their business. I'm a coach and a consultant, and I've had some success in helping various businesses with branding and social media. I don't get annoyed with the questions. I know I have complete control over how much I choose to share, and I have faith that my decision to give will have a positive effect on them and their business. I always want to be the person that others come to with questions or when they need advice on making a big decision, and my hope is that they will come to me when they need coaching or my other services, or refer someone to me. But it's not an expectation nor a requirement of being my friend or sister. Once we start to expect or demand specific results, we negate the good we may be doing. Focus on giving instead of receiving, and you'll feel empowered and full.

The First Meeting

In order to create thriving relationships and a thriving sisterhood, we have to get back to the first step in relationship building. We have to get to know each other, without any pretense or expectation. When another sister invites you out for a *"get to know you"* meeting, this should be a great time full of laughter, sharing and support. Business can be discussed, but it should never be the star of the show. By the end of that first meeting, you should know a lot more about your fellow sister, including personal details about her spouse or her kids, grandkids, perhaps a tough time she recently went through, and a bit about her hopes and dreams. I love when our sisters take pictures at their meetings and post them on social media and share how they ended up meeting for three hours. That makes my heart sing because I know they broke through that barrier and formed a true friendship that will last. Those who miss the point of this may end up having several first meetings that don't end well or result in a missed connection, usually because one of them (or both) showed up with an agenda. These kinds of meetings not only taint the potential friendship between those two sisters, but also taint the entire sisterhood. Earlier this year, we had a first time guest attend one of our evening events, Elevate. She said she had a wonderful time and was looking forward to getting to know more of the ladies. Following the event, one of our members contacted her on social media and began to "pitch" her products. They had no prior relationship before this happened, so this new potential sister was completely taken by surprise and offended. In fact, it disappointed her so much that she chose not to join our group. When the sister who originally invited her shared this insight with me, I was heartbroken. The behavior of one sister caused this potential sister to run from our group, and that's unacceptable. I did attempt to reach out to the sister who supposedly caused this, but she wasn't willing to admit any wrongdoing. A teachable moment was thwarted by pride and denial. A good rule of thumb for those reading this and wondering how to juggle a business and be a good sister is to just build the friendship first. Don't stress about the business part.

The Golf Course

If you're still reading this chapter and thinking to yourself, *"But how do I build my business, Janet?"* Okay, I hear you. Take another sip of your favorite red wine and stay with me. Think about the guys on the golf course. When men want to build relationships with other men, even with the intention of doing business with them, they often plan a golf outing. A few hours spent laughing, playing a game, and a little bit of business talk thrown in there. Guys can do this week after week, sometimes with the same guys in the golf cart. Here's what we can learn from the guys: their decision to play golf with the others isn't contingent on whether or not they do business together. Did you catch that? Even if someone chooses to not do business with the other, they still meet up the following Saturday morning for tee time. They understand that building the friendship is far more important than making the sale, and they probably understand that a "no" right now might become a "yes" later. But again, it's not expected or anticipated. It's just accepted and they move on and get to playing the game. As women, we need to approach our dealings like the guys. Form that friendship first, long before thinking how the other person needs to buy your product or service. Drop those expectations and simply be thankful for the relationship to come. Focus solely on building that relationship, and the rewards will follow. Personally, I can't stand golf. But I see the benefits of it, so that's why I'm sharing it with you.

Don't Take Everything Personally

When another sister chooses not to buy from you or do business with you, you just can't take it personally. I'm still learning this one, if I'm being completely truthful. About a year ago at one of our Empower Brunches, a fellow sister asked if anyone could help with branding and a logo. I was a bit disappointed and surprised, especially since everyone in the room knew I was a branding coach and expert. She ended up hiring a fellow sister to design her new logo, which was absolutely beautiful, but I felt hurt. Ultimately, I was happy for the other sister to receive the referral, and I was able to process my feelings of disappointment. This sister's decision of who to hire was based on her own reasons and factors, of which I will never totally understand, nor should I want to. I had to let it go and move on. I also had to remember that my mission is to build this group, not to solicit my branding business to all of them. That's never really been a goal anyway, but it's only natural to want to help others when you have a product or service that can truly benefit their life or business. But not everyone will see your value. You may do everything right, from building the friendships to being the giver, and you still may never get the business. You may not be the person they choose, for whatever reason. Remember, you can be the most beautiful and juiciest peach, but if someone just doesn't like peaches, they won't like you. It's okay, sister. Let it go.

Effing MLMs

So I debated including this part in the book. Actually, if I'm being truthful here, I wanted to devote an entire chapter to the message! Network marketing, also known as MLM or multi-level-marketing already has a bad reputation. Many of the early companies with this "pyramid structured compensation" plan created some of the horror stories we all hear about now. People were buying thousands of dollars in products, stockpiling them in their garages, hoping to sell them and make it to the top of the ranks of their companies. If we are being honest here, the data has proven that less than one percent of these poor folks are actually making money. With that being said, many of my fellow sisters are involved in network marketing and believe it's helping their families and affecting their livelihood in a positive way, so it's not my goal to discourage them from joining these companies or promoting their products. My only concern is that it is ruining our sisterhood.

Over the past few years, almost every single incident brought to my attention in the group involved network marketing. We have one sister who was sending friend requests to the family members of fellow sisters, adding hundreds of new contacts each month to widen her reach. Then the private messages start, you know the ones with all the emojis? Now before you all start composing your hate mail messages, hear me out. Why is this acceptable? I know some of these companies are teaching these tactics. *"Send friend requests to 100 people per day!"* I've stopped accepting requests from strangers. Whenever I decide to take a chance and accept them, I immediately regretted it when I get the emoji message or the *"Hey, can I send you a free sample"* message. If I don't even know you, why would I give you my mailing address and accept some strange product from you?

A couple of years ago, I decided to support a sister and try her product, a popular drink that would help me kick my die-hard soft drink habit and maybe even help me lose a few pounds. After weeks of drinking it, I was breaking out in hives and couldn't figure out why. Later I found out the drink had beet juice in it, one of my forbidden foods due to allergies. When I told my fellow sister about it, she actually responded with *"I doubt you're really allergic to that."* I was shocked. Not only did she not seem apologetic that I had a reaction, she dismissed it completely. Effing MLMs! It's causing good people to become temporarily insane and hungry for sales and money. I've seen it tear apart friendships and budding relationships. It also creates division among us, from bashing other companies' products to boasting about the purity or high quality of your own product over others. We've crossed a line, and it's time to remember there's more to life than building your downline.

Last year, my husband drank the kool-aid of one particular network marketing company and came home to convince me to help him turn this into a business. Over the next 10 months, we personally spent more than $1500 in products, attempted to recruit team members and builders, pissed off my sister-in-law and alienated a few of his old friends, and somehow felt happy when we got a commission check for $110.00. It became near impossible to try to "work the business," and it felt so icky to try to pitch our friends and family. I eventually had to let my husband know that I couldn't have my name tied to it at all. He understood and let me off the hook. Very recently, we stepped away from the company completely, for various reasons.

As I sit here, I'm drinking a protein drink from one sister's company, and sitting on my nightstand is the essential oil of another's company. In fact, I have the products of about ten sisters' businesses all over my house. I support my sisters. But it doesn't mean I have to subscribe each month for hundreds of dollars to remain their friend. That's where we've become confused. When money is involved, all bets are off. We have no idea what's going on in another sister's world, unless we've asked them about it. Spending that extra $100 per month might cause serious financial devastation for their family. We have to stop placing our monthly quotas above our sisterhood and our friendships. They are sacred and will yield far greater results than the residual income you are told will change your life. Those earnings are futile if you sacrificed your integrity to attract them. My message here isn't that network marketing is horrible and you shouldn't do it. Some of these products are excellent and are literally sitting in my very own home! My message is to do it with integrity, especially if you plan to sell anything to your fellow sisters. Just like I tell my kids, even if everyone else is doing it, it doesn't make it right. (Admit it; you've told your kids the same thing.)

RULE NINE

LEARN TO NAVIGATE CONFLICT

"Peace is not the absence of conflict;

it is the ability to handle it by peaceful means."

~Ronald Reagan

First of all, drama happens, especially when you're getting women together consistently. Ever since we were little girls running around the playground, we've been dealing with the challenges of conflict. You remember the scene; a small group of girls telling each other they are going to give one girl the silent treatment today, or they're going to pretend like they are invisible and talk to no one all day. Whatever the ridiculous reason or idea, it ends up hurting someone else. Unfortunately, this doesn't seem to improve too much as we get older, but it really should. I wish I could say that since mine is a heart-led and heart-centered organization, we do not have such problems. But that would be a lie. We still have them, but I'm determined to guide us in how we navigate them differently. Perhaps if one by one, group by group, we start to dramatically improve how we resolve conflict, it will spread to the rest of the world and start to shape us all differently. I know I sound pretty naive right now, and I'm okay with that. I know my mission is a tall one, and I know it's not for everyone. I can't allow negative thinking to derail me as I pave this path, and I don't expect anyone to pave it for me. I'm often on this road alone, and I have come to terms with that because my purpose drives me daily. And if you've been following along this far without throwing the book across the room, my guess is that you want more from your sisterhood, too.

Straight to the Source

When there's a conflict or misunderstanding, the biggest mistakes happen when the person who feels wronged chooses to go tell others instead of confronting the person who wronged them. I see this over and over again in my women's organization, and it only makes things worse. When we choose to discuss these issues with other women in the group, it may potentially taint the relationship between that person and the person you're talking about behind their back. It may result in others getting hurt by what's being said, and it tends to spread to several people before getting resolved. We have to stop this dangerous cycle. If another woman hurts your feelings or wrongs you, just pick up the phone and call her and tell her. Use those *"I statements"* we all know about and so quickly forget. Be honest and direct, but use good judgment and do not be hateful or disrespectful. Just like your grandma used to tell you, *"Two wrongs don't make a right."* Your future relationship with that person is contingent on how you handle the misunderstandings of today. Do not risk a beautiful friendship over something trivial. The reward is far greater, and the ability to resolve conflict will elevate your value in every single relationship you'll ever have or develop. I would propose this is the single most important skill to master in this life, and one that will pay off daily. Yes, sometimes confronting someone is difficult. You may sweat like a pig while you dial her number and pray the whole time she doesn't actually answer the phone. But once you do this, you are taking a huge step in the right direction. The last thing you want to do is perpetuate the issue and involve others. Avoid that like the plague. It will only poison everyone involved, and it may damage your reputation as well.

Gossip Kills

Gossip, hate, jealousy, envy and lies.

It's all around us, penetrating our friendships, networking groups and homes. Anyone reading this right now has probably seen first hand how gossip can damage your life. If you continue to engage in it, perpetuating the whispers and spreading negativity, you are only bringing more darkness upon yourself. I was visiting with a fellow sister a few months ago as we were painting pieces for the art gallery being featured at the third retreat, while chatting about life. She gave me a warning about another sister, one who has been gossiping quite a bit to others. I wasn't surprised by the person she named, but I was certainly disappointed to hear my name was one of the ones this person was talking about to others in the group. I'm the leader of the group, and somehow she is choosing to talk about me as well. It's not easy to confront these people. They often thrive on the drama, consuming it and spewing it back out to those around them. But if we keep letting them slide by with such immature and damaging behavior, we allow them to penetrate every good relationship we have built. In my organization alone, this person has been involved in numerous situations that resemble the one I described above. That's no accident.

And if, as the leader, I do not confront this and gently guide her back to the right side, it could derail the entire mission of the group. Gossip truly does kill organizations, especially the sisterhood. We have to do better. If a sister comes to you with gossip, stop her in her tracks and tell her you don't want to be a part of it. Use it as a teachable moment, and share why gossip is so dangerous. Yes it's hard. But it's important.

Intuitively escape from dark places and dark people. Your heart knows what's best.

Your Reputation Depends Upon This

If you are one of those people who thrives on gossip and drama, don't be surprised when others stop telling you anything. Once we learn who the gossipers are, we proceed with caution and avoid getting involved with the troublemaker. So if you've been stirring up drama, your reputation is probably already affected. Friends may stop inviting you to events, your business will likely suffer, and you may start feeling like everyone has abandoned you. It sounds pretty dramatic, but it truly resembles what some of my sisters have described after they came clean about being involved in gossip with other sisters. I can pretty much tell when something has happened between sisters, as I see a lot of these signs. Unfortunately, once you've created this mess, it's really hard to reverse it. It takes a lot of work and apologizing to even salvage your reputation among the others. Even if you've tried incredibly hard to make amends, you may never be able to mend the relationship with a sister you've wronged. I know it's hard to hear this, especially for those reading this who may find themselves in this situation. You have to work twice as hard to repair a broken relationship than to simply form a new one. But I want you to keep trying. Even if you mess up, apologize and do better. Your relationship with someone may never be the same, but that's not why you do it. You do it to become a better version of yourself, and hopefully, you'll learn a lesson and never do that again. Some people will never learn. That's a sad truth, and one I often have a hard time accepting because I want all of our hearts to be healed and connected. I know that about myself. It doesn't make my mission any less important. All I can do is teach and guide and pray that my words have a positive effect upon my sisters.

Stay Out of the Middle

The only place worse than being one of the two parties involved in conflict is to be the person in the middle. Somehow you have become that person who listened to both parties complain, gossip or cry about something that happened. You allowed them to tell you their side of the story, and you never put your foot down when it went too far. Instead of encouraging them to talk to each other, you inserted yourself as mediator. Now, before you start firing a bunch of excuses off to me, take a step back for a moment and think about it. When a husband and wife are having an argument, is it helpful for the mother-in-law to jump in and help them resolve it? Probably not. When we involve third parties, we only complicate matters further. Often times, the third party actually does have an allegiance to one of the parties involved, which may only be truly revealed when drama happens. This is no fun to be a part of, especially when you find out their loyalty was never to you. If you find yourself in the middle of a feud or conflict between sisters, you need to quickly remove yourself from that position. Encourage them to come together and resolve their conflict or involve a true objective third party to help. Don't let it be you because you are not objective. In fact, by the end of it, you may end up damaging your reputation with one or both of the sisters involved, simply because you played both sides. You may also become known as two-faced among the rest of the tribe, and others will steer clear of forming tight friendships with you. As a leader of a women's organization, I've seen this happen so many times. Imagine if you have a group of 100 women and about ten of these instances pop up. That's a good twenty percent of the group involved in conflict which may end up spreading to other members. It's all bad news. Don't insert yourself in the conflict between sisters. Stay out of it, for your own sake, but also for the sake of the sisterhood. Healing cannot happen if the conflict continues.

When To Involve a Leader

I've had several sisters ask me when the appropriate time to reach out to a leader might be, especially when there's conflict. Truthfully, this is a loaded question, and one I would probably answer differently every year or so. When I first founded the women's group, I wanted to know of any and all conflicts with my members, so I could help and step in whenever needed. But a couple of years into it, I realized I was doing it all wrong. First of all, I was exhausted. I was juggling phone calls and text messages left and right from sisters complaining about other sisters:

"She didn't refer me to her friend and I'm hurt."

"She cancelled our lunch meeting, and I later found out she went to lunch with another sister."

"She didn't buy my product or service."

"She told another sister that I was unhappy in my marriage, and that's none of her business."

I heard so many crazy things and accusations about fellow sisters. I would intervene when necessary, but most of the time I would encourage the sister complaining to confront the other sister directly. Truth be told, this rarely happened. I would tell them to reach out to that other sister and tell her how her actions or words hurt her, and they would nod and tell me they were going to do that. Weeks or months later, there would be another issue or complaint involving the same sisters, and I'd find out they never followed through. I used to get incredibly frustrated with this behavior. I'm ridiculously direct and straightforward. I rarely beat around the bush, and I usually don't have a filter. If someone says something offensive or hurtful to me, I speak up and address it. I don't delay, mainly because I don't want the pain or resentment to eat away at me. It's no secret that holding a grudge only damages yourself. I firmly believe that, and I've seen firsthand what happens when you can't forgive. But time and time again, I see women start to deteriorate, all because they are holding onto sadness, disappointment, resentment and anger.

So when is a good time to involve a leader in a conflict? I would say the only time to do this is when the conflict cannot be resolved between the two parties or it has affected several other sisters. For example, last year we had a sister who was involved in an issue with another sister. She found out the fellow sister had told another sister that her products (that she was heavily marketing on social media) were inferior and that no one should use them. When this got back to the original sister, she lashed out. She began calling multiple sisters and telling them about the issue. Soon, more than ten sisters were involved, and eventually, someone called me. I listened to a few sides of the story, and ultimately, reached out to the original two sisters involved. Unfortunately, so much damage had been done that the sister who was accused of sabotaging the other ended up angry and felt her reputation was badly damaged, so she left the organization altogether. I was sad to see this happen and truly felt it could have been resolved much earlier on had the original sister simply confronted her instead of waiting until it spun out of control and spewed all over the rest of the tribe. So the answer to the original question,

"When should you reach out to a leader?" I would say before it grows into a larger issue and affects more sisters.

Be Brave Enough to Apologize First

I'm not sure what's happening in our world today and why people have such a difficult time apologizing to others. We see so many messages in the media that encourage us to be "unapologetic" and "authentic," but that's not the same thing. I can be who I am meant to be, unapologetically, but I can still apologize for hurting someone's feelings. So often a sister will come to me and tell me about an incident that occurred with a fellow sister. A lot of times, it involves a text message that's been misconstrued. I can't stress enough that text messaging is a great way to deliver your message the wrong way. There are twenty different ways you can say a sentence, putting emphasis on various words to carry your point across to the reader. But some folks don't read things the same way, or perhaps English wasn't the first language they learned as a child and reading it may still be a struggle from time to time. Text messages are misunderstood all the time, and I've seen this happen in our sisterhood as well. The moment that text conversation starts to get heated, negative, accusatory or just confusing, that's a sign to pick up the phone and call. Your message is so much easier to deliver by phone. Yeah, I get it. Texting is the norm now, but take into consideration how your friendships, especially with your sisters, may be suffering due to the impersonal nature of texts. Don't risk a beautiful relationship for laziness or complacency. Dare to be different. A quick phone call can alleviate fifty texts back and forth, half of which may be misunderstood or ambiguous. I always say to avoid texting about anything that's really serious. Either call them or meet them in person. Don't assume anyone meant anything malicious initially. If you try to give them the benefit of the doubt and not jump to conclusions, it makes relationships so much easier. Always remember that holding grudges will only punish yourself. No one else usually feels it, and the other person may be completely unaware they have done something wrong. Forgiveness is a gift you give yourself. Don't allow a minor (or even a major) argument to steal your joy. Be the first to apologize and move on. Do you value that friendship? Then just swallow your pride and admit you were wrong, or admit to the part you played in the incident. Take ownership and do not be afraid to apologize. It is not a sign of weakness to apologize to others; it is a sign of strength and integrity.

Conflict can truly tear apart friendships and even the most beautiful of organizations. My motivation for writing this book is because I've seen this happen over and over again in my own sisterhood, and I want to help prevent some of these things from happening again. My purpose is to lead women to deeper connections and truly ignite within them a desire to be better than they were the day before. Being better means showing integrity, especially when shit hits the fan. It means standing up for others when they have been wronged. It means owning your part and apologizing, even if it's hard. And it means trusting your leadership when you can't handle it on your own. Do not be afraid to ask for help, but make sure it's not from someone who shouldn't be inserted directly into the middle of your conflict. Our relationships with our sisters should be sacred and protected. Choose to do the right thing and you will reap the rewards.

RULE TEN
BE A GIVER, NOT A TAKER

"Blessed are those who can give without remembering and take without forgetting."

~Elizabeth Bibesco

We've all heard this saying before:

"There are two types of people in this world, the givers and the takers..."

As I think about some of the sisters in my tribe, I have no question which category they fall into, based on their actions. If you need some help identifying your own friends, this particular rule may help you.

Givers

The givers are the first to say yes when you ask for help. They often offer selflessly to assist you and never expect anything in return. If you need a ride to an event, they are glad to carpool and refuse to accept your gas money you keep trying to shove into their hands. They don't keep a record of how many times they've helped you (or anyone else for that matter), and they are happy to help those they love. The ladies would gladly bail on their hot, bubble bath planned and meet you for a drink after a horrible day. They may surprise you with gifts, often little things they saw out shopping that just reminded them of you. When they reach out to ask to meet for coffee, it's because they genuinely want to spend time with you and never with an agenda to pitch their newest product or service. They worry they are not doing enough and are always trying to improve their relationships with fellow sisters. These people are truly making the world a better place and should be a constant reminder for all of us to be more generous and thoughtful when dealing with people in general.

Takers

The takers are not evil. Let's start there. Often times, I see someone as a taker because they have come to a place where kindness and generosity resulted in them being burned or taken advantage of, scarring them for life. They are now narrow-minded and guarded, and helping others has fallen to the bottom of their priority list. The challenge is getting these folks to forgive and release and come back to the light. Giving always makes us feel better, and we should constantly be striving to do more for our fellow sisters. Takers may show up to events with business cards in hand, ready to *"spray and pray"* as we often refer to the behavior of passing out unsolicited business cards to a large number of people. They don't ask you a single question about your life or business, and the conversation is solely about them and how *"amazing this opportunity is"* that they are currently dying to share with you. They used to understand how to build the relationship first, but lately they have forgotten. They are on a mission to recruit, sell or distribute, and the feelings or perceptions of others simply don't matter. The ironic thing about this is that they have no idea they are now considered a taker. If someone clued them in on that fact, they would act surprised. They don't even see it that way. They just see themselves on a mission, out to achieve everything they deserve! From experience with these types of people, many of them wake up eventually and realize they've been isolating themselves or avoiding friends. That's usually the first sign. They may admit to being hurt in the past and confess they have built a bit of a wall around their hearts. If you ask me (which technically you are since you agreed to read this book) takers can always become givers. It's all cyclical. We go through seasons in our lives when we fall into one category more than the other. Sometimes we give and give and give, and then we breakdown and just stop for a while.

If you have identified someone in your life as a taker, I would encourage you to maintain the friendship, unless it's abusive in some way. Continue to nurture them. Gently remind them at times when they are being selfish or overly guarded. Sometimes a friendly face and a gentle hand can guide us back to the good side. Don't dismiss these sisters either, unless they've given you a good reason to do so. They may need love. Listen to your heart and not your ego when you're truly trying to make a difference in the life of another person. The ego is all about self-preservation.

RULE ELEVEN
PUT THE DAMN PHONE DOWN

"I fear the day that technology will surpass our human interaction. The world will have a generation of idiots."

~Albert Einstein

I get it. We are all addicted to our fancy smartphones. They do everything we need them to do, from managing contacts and calendars, to helping us shop and pay bills. With so many updates, upgrades and changes, our phones are capable of doing more and more each and every year. We can ask it for the weather update, have it text someone as we dictate exactly what we want the message to say, and even have reminders pop up the moment we pull into our driveway at home. My husband talks to his phone constantly, even calling it names when it doesn't get his Google search correct. Yes, it's comical at times, but it's eliminated the necessary steps we used to take to search for information and talk to people.

While these phones may be smart and super savvy, they are preventing us from being in the moment. Every event I walk into, I see men and women standing in corners, their faces glued to their phones. One woman I recently saw outside a networking event looked so enthralled in her phone that I assumed she was answering an important email or dealing with a sick child or something serious because she just had that intentional look on her face the whole time. But when I casually strolled by her, she was playing a serious game of Candy Crush. I'm not kidding, y'all. This lady was missing out on networking completely, all to crush some candy and win points that never really matter.

If you are showing up to an event, turn your cell phone to silent or vibrate and slip it into your purse. I wear a Fitbit on my wrist, so if my phone is silently ringing in my purse, I know who is calling. I also don't have to take out my phone and check it constantly. If there's an emergency, they will likely call more than once. Are we really that important that we can't have an hour without our phones? It's time to remember our manners and put the damn phones away.

Small Talk is Gone

These damn phones have taken over the small talk opportunities in our lives. Remember years ago when you were waiting in line at the grocery store or stuck in an elevator with another person? You naturally chatted with them for a few minutes about the weather or may have even made a new friend. In today's world, those moments are completely missed. We never look up from our phones, so we never strike up that conversation. I was recently sitting with someone for a first time coffee meeting, and she began to login and check her email during a story I was telling. I was pretty shocked and even confronted her about her behavior. She laughed nervously at me and then replied with, *"Don't we all check our email constantly?"* No. No we don't, Susan. And you don't have to either. Not only is it incredibly rude, I highly doubt the latest Nordstrom sale is urgent enough to completely ignore a potential referral source or business partner. Are we really this distracted? The only exception is if you are dealing with an emergency, such as a sick child or relative in the hospital. If that's the case, state it upfront and let it be known, perhaps with a disclaimer such as, *"Hey, my aunt is in the hospital and I'm waiting on some urgent news."* People respect that. Also make sure you're being truthful. Don't use lies as excuses. With social media, it's easy to be "outed" when you tell a fib.

Important Conversations in Text

I've already covered parts of this, but don't use text messaging as a way to handle delicate or serious conversations. If you aren't sure how someone might react to a question or request, that should be a clear sign that it's inappropriate to send via text. Now, the exception to this might be if this person is known for gossip, or perhaps one of those people who tend to twist conversations and spread lies about what might have really been said. With those types of people, I tend to put everything in writing, to cover myself and protect my reputation. But if we're talking about a friend, sister or potential business partner (with no prior miscommunications), just pick up the phone if there's a serious conversation. Texts are always misunderstood and misconstrued. You can read a sentence ten different ways, putting emphasis on a different word every time you read it. That's what happens when your text comes through, and the recipient doesn't understand it. They re-read it over and over again, changing the tone and inflection until they think they know what you meant. It's a great way to completely screw up a friendship, so just avoid that at all costs. We've lost the art of just picking up the phone. So many claim, "I just don't like talking on the phone." But seriously, you could have a ten-minute conversation and clearly relay your thoughts and emotions, or spend days trying to apologize and reiterate what you really meant in your text messages. And if you already offended them, forget it. The damage has been done, and it will take twice as many texts to fix it. Trust me. Call them.

Social Media 101

Since we're on the subject of smartphones and miscommunication, let's chat about social media. I see so many inappropriate messages posted on Facebook or Instagram. Blame it on generational differences, cultural differences or whatever, but let's have a real conversation about what we should be sharing in a public forum on a daily basis.

Female Issues

First of all, I sympathize with you, Sister, if you have period problems. I struggled for many years with various issues, until finally undergoing a hysterectomy at age 29. But Facebook is not where we need to share all of that. Posting about our PCOS, irregular periods, ruined jeans, or anything related to female stuff really isn't necessary.

Would you walk into a coffee shop and announce this to the patrons? If not, then it should definitely not be posted on social media for all to see. The exception to this one might be in a private group where you're interacting with like-minded women. I get that.

Marriage Issues

I'm on my second marriage. After failing miserably on what I now refer to as my "starter marriage," I'm truly blessed to have found the love of my life, a special education teacher named Harold. He's amazing and treats me like a queen. We are, however, a real-life couple, with real-life marriage problems. He is pretty forgetful, and he falls asleep during our favorite shows we are binge-watching on Netflix, sometimes as early as 7:30pm. Of course, this is usually the result of getting up extra early to go to the gym, combined with a stressful and physical job of being a phenomenal special education teacher who specializes in non-verbal children, Autistic children and even adolescents with behavior issues. So even though his falling asleep early may drive me mad, I avoid sharing negative relationship comments on social media at all costs. It's just not the place, not to mention I do not want to be that wife. You know the one? She only posts complaints. No matter how wonderful their 10-day vacation to Jamaica was last month, and how much she adores their five gorgeous children, she bashes him in front of everyone for forgetting to take the trash out. Don't be her. It's not flattering for anyone. I laugh as I write this, because my sweet husband just asked me, *"If you aren't supposed to share it to social media, is it better to write it in a book for (potentially) millions to read?"* Oh honey...

Vague-Booking

You know what this is. It's your bestie who posts a vague status update that simply says, "Unspoken prayer request" or "I have a secret!" For those of us who are truly empathetic, we can't stand this. If we are being asked to pray for you, at least tell us something to pray for, or provide some sort of detail. If you can't give any details, don't post that vague post! Just stop. Most of the time, it's simply to attract attention. I'll be honest; I've done it, too. This part of the book is speaking to me as well. We all need to do better. Also avoid those posts that are clearly ABOUT someone else, but you don't give enough information to identify them. It's pretty much called passive-aggressive, but we all just sit back and wait for the person you're talking about to find the post. I did this last year, too. I hosted a surprise birthday event, only the guest of honor never showed up. I posted something on

Facebook like, *"When you throw a surprise party and they never show up."* It got back to the person I was referring to, and she got her feelings hurt. I learned a shitty lesson, and I won't do it again. We post this type of stuff because we seek validation or confirmation. Either way, we have to be better.

Politics or Religion

Once again, refer back to the new rule "Be Inclusive," where I talk about the Bermuda Triangle. When we start posting hateful rhetoric, especially bashing other religions or political candidates, we alienate our friends and family. We trigger knee-jerk reactions and often ones that aren't pleasant and sacrifice all the time we've spent building a friendship as our impulsive words tear it down. It's just not worth it. If you love Jesus, post positive quotes or verses. But don't bash other religions. And if you're wearing a bracelet that says, *"What Would Jesus Do?"* I can tell you he wouldn't be bashing his Jewish friends or Buddhist friends on Facebook, nor would he be spewing his opinions on homosexuality or abortion all over his news feed. We have to stop using our beliefs to justify our inappropriate actions. Just stop, girlfriend. Our mission here in this world should be to love, not hate. No matter your religion, I think the ultimate message is to spread love and not hate. If your religion teaches you to hate anyone, you need a new religion. These can be incredibly personal beliefs and ones that have been instilled in us from a very young age. Sometimes we feel personally attacked when someone attacks a belief we hold dear. If you genuinely are passionate about something, always ask yourself if someone close to you might be offended or heartbroken if you stood up and spoke about it. Often times we are passing judgment when we don't have any authority to do so. I'm going to go more into judgment in the next rule, but always take a step back and ask yourself, *"Who might be hurt by this post or comment?"* If it's anyone you care about, just refrain.

Food Pictures

Just kidding. We all love those posts, even if we say we don't. Keep posting the pictures of your dinners and drinks, unless they feature kale.

Social media is a wonderful tool, and one that can nurture relationships with your sisters and friends. It's a great way to connect with each other, cheer each other on and deepen relationships. But as with any tool, it all depends on how you use it. Abusing social media can lead to miscommunications, hurt feelings, alienation and more. Be conscious of how you're showing up online, and if you find yourself in a coffee shop with another sister, put the damn phone down.

RULE TWELVE
MORE EMPATHY, LESS JUDGMENT

"Every criticism, judgment, diagnosis and expression of anger is the tragic expression of an unmet need."

~Marshall B. Rosenberg

I saved the new rules on judgment for last, so if I piss you off too much, hopefully I've already made an impression throughout the rest of the book. I'm sort of kidding. I know the topic of judgment is a sticky one. We all judge to some extent, and some of what I'm about to share might strike a nerve with many.

We have no right to judge anyone.

Yep, that's how I'm starting this one. We all love to brag about our rights, citing the various amendments that back up our stance. We don't hesitate to throw that age old phrase, *"To each his own"* when we hear about someone living life a different way than we would. But that's not where it stops. We don't just mutter that phrase and walk away. The trouble starts when we pass judgment on that same person's life choices or decisions.

In the Name of Religion

I live in Texas, also known as an integral part of the so-called "Bible Belt" of America. There's a church on every corner and about fifty different denominations of Christianity. I grew up in the Christian church and even found myself in the role of a praise and worship leader, sharing my voice on stage every Sunday. I loved being a part of a church community and thought I had forged deep friendships with these like-minded people. Boy was I wrong. The moment I announced my divorce, I was plucked from the stage and removed as a leader in the church. I was told if I didn't reconcile with my husband, I was not going to receive the blessings of God upon me. Wow, thanks Pastor. I'm sharing this not because I think church is bad. I still cling to my faith, and that has not waivered. But if your religion measures the sin of its members, it might be time to re-evaluate your religion. We all sin and fall short. None of us are perfect. If there's an excel spreadsheet showing which sins are acceptable and which are forbidden, I missed that course in Sunday School. It clearly states in the Bible, *"Thou shalt not judge,"* and again in another chapter, *"Judge not, lest you be judged."* That second verse is actually referring more to the hypocrisy of judging another when you have done the same thing. Either way, we are reminded over and over again that we are not the judge.

If you engage in a weekly Bible study group, be certain you are studying the Bible and not engaging in gossip about other women. Another woman's lifestyle, decisions or challenges should NEVER become the topic of discussion in such a setting. Any leader in this kind of group should always be aware of the appearance of such topics should they leak out (and they always do.)

For the record, whatever you may believe does not personally matter to me. If you think that homosexuality is a choice, I'm not going to start an argument with you. If you believe that only selfish women choose abortion, that's not a fight in which I'm happy to participate. But the moment you use religion to justify judgment, that's where it ends. If you want to be a part of a thriving sisterhood, you are either supporting the mission or creating division. We all know the controversial subjects, and we should all know by now to avoid them or tread incredibly lightly. It's time we stopped spewing intolerance because we truly have no right to judge!

Are you still here?

I'm checking in now, since I know I went a little "preachy," for lack of a better word.

Seriously, who are we to judge others? Have we been ordained by an authority and given the green light to approve or disapprove our fellow sisters? Did we wake up one morning with a magical wand that lights up and allows us to prance around and announce to the world who is good and who is bad?

No, that's not the case.

We are all human. We are all going to make mistakes. But our decision to judge or condemn another sister is just wrong. And gathering a group of fellow sisters to pass judgment together is only going to tear apart the women we are called to love.

Stop Perpetuating the Mental Health Stigma

If I'm being totally transparent, this was not in the original draft of this book. I finished the manuscript and sent it to my editors and assumed I was pretty much done with the book. Two days later, I found out an old friend I had worked with more than ten years ago had died by suicide. Her name was Caitlin Ussery Staten, and she was only 32 years old. She was truly one of the most caring and generous souls I'd ever met, and I had no idea she was struggling with depression. I sat in her somber memorial service where she was remembered and honored for who she was and the joy she brought to so many lives, including hundreds of rescue dogs she saved, transported, fostered and loved. I cried and cried over the loss of such a beautiful person and for the devastating effects it had upon her family she left behind. I began to judge myself, asking why I had lost touch with her over the past couple of years. I beat myself up, wondering if I could have helped her had I known. I wondered if having a tribe like mine could have helped her and prevented her decision to take her own life. I knew these thoughts weren't productive, but I couldn't shake the feeling of regret. I was determined to raise awareness for suicide and make sure I started looking for 'signs' in my own friends and loved ones.

On February 25th, just a week after Caitlin's memorial service, a dear Heart Sister and friend also died by suicide. Shelley Storm was part of The Every Heart Project's leadership team, serving as our Vice President of Membership. She was the epitome of what a Heart Sister truly is, her generosity and compassion known by so many of our members. She was always the one to volunteer to help a sister in need, help set up for an event, and even donate money to secretly sponsor sisters who wanted to attend retreats and couldn't cover the entire cost. She gave and gave and loved with her whole heart. When I found out the news about Shelley, I fell apart. I sat alone at my desk in my home office, tears streaming down my face. I began to replay every text message, phone call and memory involving my dear friend. How did I miss the signs? Were there obvious clues that could have shown me she needed help? I cancelled most of my appointments for the week to allow myself time to grieve and process this immense loss. I spent many hours in prayer and juggling texts, phone calls and messages from fellow sisters who were doing the same. Our community felt this loss on a deep level, and it hurt to the core. That following Saturday, many of us showed up to attend the funeral service. It was one of the toughest funerals I had been to, and my heart ached the entire time. We all pitched in to purchase a heart-shaped floral arrangement, and many of us offered support to the family. It was probably the toughest thing I've had to face as a leader in my life.

Just a few days prior to the funeral, our monthly Every Heart Sisters evening event (Elevate) was scheduled to take place. Instead of the usual programming, I tossed it all out and decided to devote the night to Shelley's memory and education about suicide, depression and how to support each other. It was a really difficult night, but it was also gorgeous in a way. Many of our sisters shared memories of dear Shelley, of her devotion to helping others and how she exhibited love in everything she did. Some opened up about their own depression and anxiety and how hard days can be when you are suffering through it. We discussed how to best support each other during the darkest days and how to recognize when someone might need help. At the end of the evening, I sang 'Go Rest High On That Mountain' and announced the Shelley Storm Scholarship Fund. Because the one thing she most loved to do was donate anonymously to her fellow sisters, we felt it was fitting to create a fund to further her memory. Her beautiful face will forever be remembered on our website, for the life of the project, and may we never forget to reach out to those in need.

Regardless of your opinions on mental illness, medication or treatment, we need to stop perpetuating the stigma of mental illness. If our fellow sisters are suffering, they need to know it's safe to open up and share how they are feeling. If they are discouraged from doing so, they will be forced to struggle in silence, creating more isolation and sadness. We have to stop this vicious cycle before we lose anyone else. I urge you to wrap your arms around the women in your own circle, especially those who suffer from anxiety, depression or any other mental illness. They need our love more than ever, and the sisterhood can never thrive without this final component.

Sadly, some of the most supportive sisters in our tribe felt as though writing about this topic or remembering these beautiful souls meant we were glorifying suicide and mental illness. Although that is certainly not the intent, I am heartbroken this is how such issues are still being treated. It all goes back to the stigma of mental illness. We need to do better. How someone died should not taint how we remember their lives. Once again, more empathy and less judgment is the final rule for a reason.

CONCLUSION

These are the new rules of the Sisterhood. These rules are not meant to anger anyone or alienate anyone. If you felt conviction while reading any part of this, I encourage you to lean into that feeling and ask yourself how you can use this as a teachable moment and self-correct your behavior. None of us are perfect, and we are not called to be so. When we do something wrong or hurt another sister's feelings, we have an opportunity to rise up and make it right. We have a choice to pick up the phone and deliver a heartfelt apology or invite her out for coffee and ask for forgiveness. In our society, where we have become selfie-obsessed and *"all about me"* driven, it's time we set aside our personal desires and place our relationships first.

In the Sisterhood, we are only as strong as our relationships. If those are not thriving, we are merely surviving and never truly living the mission. If gossip, judgment, lies and hate are filling our news feeds, it's time we unfollowed and unsubscribed. Just say no to anything that contradicts our calling to love our sisters.

If your religion requires you to hate a group of people, find a new religion.

If your political party requires you to hate the other side, ask yourself why you blindly follow.

If your female friendships are best described as tumultuous, take a step back and ask yourself what kind of behaviors are taking place. Are lunches and coffee dates filled with negativity, trash talk and judgment? Is there always a miscommunication resulting in silent treatment or gossip? Do you truly feel uplifted and empowered after spending time with these friends? Or do you feel drained, disappointed or depressed? Do an inventory of your closest friends and those with whom you spend the most time. Are they givers or takers? Are they empathetic or judgmental?

The only way to create a tribe that thrives is to make the hard decisions to be better.

YOUR TURN

Thank you for joining me on this journey!

Although this is meant to be a non-threatening, somewhat lighthearted 'guide' for us as women, I also want to challenge you to rebuild and restore the friendships in your circle by implementing these rules.

In order to create a new, thriving Global Sisterhood we all have to step up and make this commitment. So, if you are ready to make a difference in the world, I need your help.

Head over to Facebook and find our group: The New Rules of the Sisterhood Book Club. Join a community of women who are striving daily to live by the new rules and rebuild and restore friendships. We can do this, Sisters, but we all have to do this together.

Join me there, as I encourage you, guide you and inspire you to be your most authentic self and chase those audacious dreams! I believe all women are capable of so much more, and I'd love to engage with you in our new group to further this mission.

See you there! #NewRules #SisterhoodRules

www.EveryHeartProject.com/sisterhood

IN LOVING MEMORY OF:

Shelley Storm

November 16, 1965 - February 25, 2019

And

Caitlin Marie Ussery Staten

February 7, 1986 - January 30, 2019

"I think the saddest people always try their hardest

to make people happy because they know

what it feels like to feel absolutely worthless

and they don't want anyone else to feel like that."

~Robin Williams

National Suicide Prevention Lifeline: 800-273-TALK (8255)

SuicidePreventionLifeline.org

ABOUT THE AUTHOR

Janet Bernstein is the founder of Savvy Girl Media as well as a best-selling author of five books, including her memoir *"Pizza On The Floor,"* a story of growing up with a mother with Borderline Personality Disorder. As a Visibility Coach, she empowers women entrepreneurs to pursue their dreams and show up authentically online and in person. She left a 17-year career in the corporate insurance world in 2015 to pursue her own dream of becoming an author, speaker and champion of women. In 2014, she began leading women's groups and eventually founded The Every Heart Project, designed to connect women from the heart. Their mission is to empower, elevate and equip women for success, and her local Dallas, Texas chapter is where she proudly hosts at least two events per month, including writing and speaking workshops, book studies, how-to technology workshops and more. She is also a mom of three, stepmom to two bonus daughters, and happily married to her partner for life, an amazing special education teacher, Harold. They reside in Carrollton, Texas with their family, along with two rescue pups and a sassy cat named Nikita.

Learn more at:

EveryHeartProject.com

SavvyGirlMedia.com

Made in the USA
Columbia, SC
31 March 2019